*Alice —
The memoirs
in back are some of
Shawn's erotic stories —*

A LAP AROUND ALASKA
An AlCan Adventure

SHAWN INMON

A Lap Around Alaska
By Shawn Inmon

©2017 by Shawn Inmon

All rights reserved.

This book or parts thereof may not be reproduced in any form, stored in or introduced into a retrieval system, or transmitted, in any form, or by any means (electronic, mechanical, photocopying, recording, or otherwise) without prior written permission of the copyright owner and/or publisher of this book, except as provided by United States of America copyright law.

The views expressed in this work are solely those of the author.

All photographs copyright 2017, Shawn Inmon

Cover Design/Interior Design: Linda Boulanger
Tell~Tale Book Covers

Published by Pertime Publishing

Also available in eBook publication

PRINTED IN THE UNITED STATES OF AMERICA

For Mick
I owe you so much
for opening my eyes to Alaska.

I want to start by telling you what kind of book this is and, almost as important, what it *isn't*. This book isn't a travel guide in which I attempt to tell you everything there is to know about British Columbia, Yukon, and Alaska. There are a lot of those books available, *The Milepost* being the gold standard. Guide books are great for providing information on things to see, hotels, restaurants, and so forth. That's helpful, of course, but they don't always describe what it's like to actually be there.

That's what I will try to convey in this book: what it felt like, in the early spring of 2017, to drive north through British Columbia, across the Yukon territory on the Alaska Highway, then drive a loop around south-central Alaska. I'll mention some specific sites and drives, of course, but I will do my best to share them through one traveler's eyes, essentially inviting you along with me on the drive.

If you are planning your own trip over the Alaska Highway and around the Last Frontier, I do recommend grabbing the most recent edition of *The Milepost*. It's a thorough, informative travel guide that will tell you everything you need to know to plan a trip. If you're wondering what it would be like to actually take that journey, though, I hope you'll come with me on my own *Lap Around Alaska*.

Why Alaska?

Why leave my comfy home on the Pacific coast of southern Washington and venture up the Alaska Highway, then drive a huge loop around the America's largest state??

So many reasons. There is certainly no other state like Alaska. The sheer size is impressive, yes, but there is much more to the state than its overwhelming heft. There's the scenery, of course—unmatched anywhere in the United States, in my opinion. There's the wildlife, too. On a given day, you might see bear, moose, bald eagles, otters, dolphins, foxes, mountain goats, whales, or caribou. Don't forget the solitude that also can be found in Alaska, an unusual commodity in today's world. As much as any of these, though, the people are something special.

I drove a similar "lap" around the height and breadth of the lower 48 states last year, and I met dozens of fascinating people. In my experience, Alaskans—both natives to the state and people who have been drawn there—are a breed apart: iconoclasts, satisfied with who they are, who don't much care what you or I think of them. I'll admit it: I love Alaskans.

The very first man I spoke to when I crossed from Canada into Alaska told me, "There's a couple things you should know. We don't have a city government here, and that's the way we like it. Also, just assume that every person you meet is armed, and you'll be right more often than you're wrong. Act accordingly." I try to act in such a fashion that people, armed or not, do not want to kill me on sight, but I appreciated the advice.

All those reasons aside, I had personal reasons, too. When I was fourteen years old, my big brother sent me a plane ticket to come spend the summer with him in Alaska. He did the same thing for the next two summers. Those three trips to Alaska were the highlight of my childhood. While there, I got to serve as a cook and deckhand on a crabber called the Diver I. I worked as a short-order cook the next summer, even though I still didn't have the foggiest idea how to cook. It's amazing what you can fake your way through, if you have just a little chutzpah. My final summer in Alaska was spent camping out with my brother in the Matanuska Valley, trying to nurture a bag full of seeds into a cash crop of marijuana. The financial end of that summer didn't work out at all well, but the months spent camping out with my brother were sublimely happy.

After those idyllic summers in the '70s, Alaska was deep in my soul, but I'd never been back. It was time to remedy that.

Finally, there is the lure of the Alaska Highway, which I will often refer to as the AlCan, short for Alaska-Canada Highway. Driving from one end of it to the other is the kind of adventure that I find irresistible.

In all, the trip lasted twenty-two days, and, as all epic road trips do, changed who I am and what I think, at least a little.

Unlike the tour chronicled in *A Lap Around America*, my beautiful bride, Dawn, did not accompany me on this lap around Alaska, for several reasons. For one, she's never been as bitten by the travel bug as I am. For her, a trip should include swimming pools, sunshine, and possibly a spa. This trip around Alaska offered none of those things. More important, we had a new granddaughter set to arrive in this world late in May. If she decided to make an early appearance, we didn't want both of us to be thousands of miles away.

So, this is the story of a solo lap. But of course, it's really not. The front seat is empty and waiting for you.

Preparation

Typically, I don't do a lot of prep work for my road trips. On our *Lap Around America*, I basically bought a few road maps and a comprehensive book on the national parks, and off we went. Driving around the Lower 48 is much different from traveling the oft-deserted highways of British Columbia, Yukon, and Alaska.

Also, when we drove around America, it was in a brand new car we had dubbed The Silver Bullet. For this trip, I would be chugging along in my 1997 Subaru Outback wagon, with more than 115,000 miles under its wheels. As Subaru owners know, though, an Outback is just starting to hit its stride when the odometer clicks over the 100,000 mark. I bought this car four years ago, when it had 65,000 miles on it. Since then, all I'd ever done to her was change the oil. She'd never given me a lick of trouble.

Nonetheless, I pictured those long stretches of road that carry few vehicles and have no cellphone service. I didn't want to break down on one of those lonely stretches. So, I took her to my trusted local shop in Seaview and asked the mechanic to look at every belt and hose and to replace any that looked even fifty percent worn. After that, I put four new tires on.

Did I do a lot of research about Alaska? No, of course not. I did order a copy of the 2017 *Milepost*, which is *de rigueur* for every Alaskan traveler, but that was the extent of my research. Truth be told, I didn't even crack open my *Milepost* until I was already on the road. I like to take things as they come and be open to the experiences a road trip has to offer.

I packed up our old Magical Mystery Bag with sandwich makings, trail mix, and granola bars, and then I was ready to roll. Next stop: British Columbia.

Day One

I left on this trip in mid-April. I mention this so you can have at least some idea of what to expect in terms of weather and what facilities might be open for the season if you leave around the same time. In the days ahead, I found a large number of businesses still shuttered for winter. Had I left thirty days later, they would probably have been open.

If this is your first trip riding shotgun with me, you should know the rules I abide by:

1. Avoid freeways wherever possible. Back roads, the more remote the better, are the order of the day. This is, admittedly, easier in Alaska.

2. Avoid corporations wherever possible. I can get Subway or Applebee's food within easy driving distance of my house. Ditto with chain hotels. On a road trip, I want to eat in small cafes and stay in roadside motels.

Aside from those simple rules, my only goal is to see as much of the local culture as possible, and to take advantage of whatever opportunities the road puts in front of me.

I had planned on getting an early start on day one. I am an early riser, wide awake by 6 a.m. But this day I dawdled a bit. Now that the time had arrived to go, I found myself reluctant to leave Dawn. We've been married for six and a half years and have rarely spent more than a night apart. With the reality of three weeks or more of sleeping alone in tiny roadside motels upon me, both home and Dawn looked more attractive than ever.

Dawn and I already had a joint history with Alaska. During my senior year in high school, I had planned to spend the summer before college in Alaska with my best friend, Jerry. We were hoping to catch on with the crabber on which my brother Mick was a deckhand.

Then, after being friend-zoned and girlfriendless my entire life, a miracle happened that spring. Dawn and I, close friends for years, fell in love. Suddenly, the trip to Alaska—which had once seemed a grand adventure with my best friend—was looking like a long, lonely stretch without the girl I loved. I wasn't mature enough to handle the situation, so Jerry and I went to Alaska. And I was miserable. Things were very different in 1978, of course—no Internet, no cellphones, no easy way to stay in touch with each other. Dawn and I were in the indescribable throes of first love, which manages to push any other thought from your head. Instead of staying the three months I had planned, I flew home after a week and a half.

Now, almost 40 years later, I still get a little twitterpated around Dawn, but I think I'll manage to make it through the whole trip this time.

By 9 a.m., I had delayed as long as I could, and the Emerald Bullet and I, pointed north, rolled out of the driveway. Avoiding freeways meant a much longer, slower drive on Day One. The easy route to Canada from Seaview is to stay on Highway 101 all the way to Interstate 5 in Olympia, then take that massive freeway all the way to the border. That makes for a quick but not lovely drive. All that traffic up the I-5 corridor can ruin your day.

I've made the first hour of this drive—leaving Long Beach, driving along Willapa Bay—dozens, if not hundreds, of times. Still, I did my best to look at it with fresh eyes. Much of that first hour was spent with Willapa Bay on my left and fir-covered hills on my right. Looking at it from a new perspective reminded me how fortunate I am to live here, surrounded by green, low-lying hills, saltwater and fresh air.

Two hours into the drive, just when it felt as though I was getting close to more dense civilization, I took the McCleary cutoff to Highway 108, and found myself immediately in a part of my own state that I did not recognize. I've lived in Washington for all but a few of my fifty-seven years, but there are still areas that I've visited rarely. As I drove past Kamilche and Skokomish, I knew I had made a mistake by ignoring the area. All of the western half of the state is green, but this area takes that to an extreme. Deep emerald jewels of color surrounded me.

It had been raining lightly ever since I left home, but that's a fairly permanent proposition in Western Washington in April. I reconnected with Highway 101 north and drove alongside the western shore of Hood Canal. Fog settled over the area, so thick that I dropped my speed down to under the posted limit.

Tried to shoot the fog, but I mist

Highway 101 between Hoodsport and Quilcene is a lovely scenic drive—Hood Canal on your right, the deep greens of the Olympic National Forest on your left. Had this been just a day trip, I would have been pulling over constantly to breathe in that clean air and feel the crunch of needles under my shoes. But I was on a mission to make it across the Canadian border on the first day, so I pushed on.

My plan was to make it to Port Townsend by noon, then catch the ferry across Admiralty Bay to Whidbey Island and then make Canada by dinnertime. Shawn plans, God laughs.

I actually got to Port Townsend a little earlier than anticipated, so I took my first mini side trip. Port Townsend is a picture-postcard kind of town, combining a century-old maritime heritage and vintage architecture with a sense of style and artistic chic. The harbor rings the town, giving it an authentic maritime vibe, while small, artsy shops dot the town itself. It's the kind of place where you can easily spend a day wandering the streets and investigating shops. It's also the home of Fort Worden State Park, which is what interested me.

Fort Worden State Park served as the primary shooting site for the movie *An Officer and a Gentleman*, starring Richard Gere and Debra Winger. You might recognize this spot, which was used as a shooting location for many of the training sequences in that movie:

Fort Worden State Park

Beyond being the filming location for a well-known '80s movie, Fort Worden also carries personal meaning for me. It's where I started the journey that would eventually lead to becoming a full-time author. In 1975, I was fifteen years old. A contest was launched to find Washington's Most Promising Young Writers. My English teacher, Dennis Merz, encouraged me to enter a short story. The winners from around the state got to spend three days and nights at Fort Worden, working with published authors, learning to hone our fledgling skills.

When Mr. Merz first told me about the contest, I had months to write the story. As much as I wanted to skip three days of school to attend the conference, my ability to procrastinate was unmatched, even at that early date. Eventually, Mr. Merz said, "If you want to enter a story in that contest, I'll need it on my desk by tomorrow." I hadn't written a single word. In fact, I didn't even have an idea for a story.

I went home, got out our old manual Royal typewriter, and sat staring at a blank page for an hour or so, waiting for inspiration. At that moment, my friend Mark knocked on the door and asked if I wanted to come outside and hang out. Since the alternative was a continued sinking feeling in the pit of my stomach as I stared at that damn blank page, of course I did!

When I met Mark in the yard, I saw he was holding a weird sort of ball. It was about six inches across, made of soft, pliant rubber, and had small round handles that protruded in half a dozen spots. We played catch with the ball for a while, but, being teenage boys, we began throwing it harder and harder, trying to smack each other with it. That evolved into a war game of sorts, in which whoever had the ball used it as a weapon to track down and "kill" the other. Boys are so naturally violent.

Eventually, Mom called me inside for the night and I saw the typewriter sitting forlornly at our kitchen table. In an instant, I saw a story in my mind. I sat down at the table, and two hours later, I had my story written. It was set in the firebombed city of Dresden, where there were only two remaining soldiers alive—one German and one American. They hunted each other through the city until they came face to face in the city square. For reasons I'm not quite clear on all these years later, they abandoned their rifles and engaged in hand-to-hand combat for a few moments, until they glanced to the side and saw a small, ragged girl, holding a torn dolly in her hand. They looked at each other, realized the inhumanity of trying to kill the only other adult left alive in the town, and turned and walked away from each other, toward their own destinies. Not exactly historically accurate, but what did I know? I was fifteen.

I turned the story in to Mr. Merz and forgot about it, until a month later when he told me I had been named one of those "promising young writers" who had been chosen to go to Fort Worden. Forty years later, I still carry many of the lessons I learned at that conference with me when I sit down to find another blank page waiting to be filled.

I drove through and tried to remember which building I had been assigned to back then. Everything looked unchanged after forty years, a rare experience in itself.

I checked the time and saw that it was 12:15. There was a ferry that left Port Townsend at 12:30, and I wondered if I could make it. Five minutes later, I was at the gate.

A bored lady slid her window open and said, "Yes, can I help you?" Since we were sitting at the gate to the ferry dock, I thought it was fairly obvious what I wanted, but I cleared the air by saying, "I need a ticket to Coupeville. Do you think I can get on the 12:30 ferry?" I looked ahead and saw that the ferry hadn't arrived yet.

She sucked her teeth and whistled slowly. "Not sure if we'll get you on the 12:30. You should make the 2 o'clock with no trouble, though."

There are worse things in life than parking on a dock and walking around a beautiful town like Port Townsend. Besides, what else was I going to do, backtrack all the way to Olympia? I bought the ticket and pulled into the lane she pointed out.

A few minutes later, the ferry to Whidbey Island arrived, and, sure enough, I didn't make it on. No worries. I got out of the car and took a nice long walk along the water, smelling the sea air and watching the birds. I got back to the Emerald Bullet just a few minutes before 2 p.m. and climbed inside, ready to continue the journey.

The 2 p.m. ferry arrived, loaded, and departed. I sat without moving. I did a little math in my head. The next ferry wouldn't be until 3:30. Making Canada by dinner was looking like a pipe dream.

I got out of the car once again and walked back to the lady who had sold me the ticket. "Hello," I said, with a slightly forced smile. "I bought a ticket a couple of hours ago."

She met my fixed smile with one of her own, but didn't say anything. I could see I was going to have to carry the momentum of the conversation.

"When I did, you said I would make the 2 o'clock with no trouble, but it just came and went."

She nodded. My logic was unassailable.

"Did I do something wrong? What do I need to do to catch the ferry?"

"Did you make a reservation?"

"No, I just pulled up and you sold me a ticket."

She nodded out at the departing ferry, filled with people happily making their way to Coupeville, taking my hope of keeping on schedule with them. "They had reservations."

"So, even though I bought a ticket and was waiting here for several hours, they load people with reservations first?"

"Yes," she said, as though she couldn't believe I was so dense.

Perhaps I was.

"Can I make a reservation now?"

"Certainly, sir, but you'll need to leave the lot and get a refund on the ticket you bought. Then, you can make a reservation and get back in line."

"Is that what you would do? I just want to make sure I catch the next ferry."

"If I was you," she said with some authority, once again sucking her teeth, "I would just sit right where you are."

I know when I am beaten. I went back to the car, plucked my copy of *The Milepost 2017* from the seat, and spent the next 90 minutes dreaming of Alaska, which seemed very far away.

Finally, the 3:30 ferry arrived. The cars that were filled with people who understood the labyrinthine rules of the Washington State Ferry System, all of whom had arrived in the past fifteen minutes, started to load. I was worried that I was going to once again sit, unmoving, as the ferry left. Just then, though, a man in an orange safety vest moved to the front of my row and flagged us toward the ferry.

Four cars until I boarded. Three. Two. I was next.

The man in the orange vest held up a hand, smiled, then placed an orange cone in front of me. He turned and walked away.

In disbelief, I watched the ferry pull away from the dock.

I called Dawn.

"How's the trip?" she answered, chipper and happy.

"I think I'm turning around and coming home."

"What?" She knew I was sometimes prone to exaggeration, as every storyteller is.

I recounted my adventure in trying to board the ferry, then promised her, "If I don't make it on the next, I really am turning around and coming home. I'll leave again tomorrow." At that moment, the idea of lying on my soft bed, Dawn beside me, looking out on the trees of our backyard with the sounds of the ocean coming through the window, seemed heavenly.

After ninety minutes of stewing in my own juices and making myself miserable, I managed to get on the 5 p.m. ferry. My blood pressure returned to something approaching normal as soon as I felt the rocking waves beneath my feet. What's five wasted hours on an epic road trip? A drop in the bucket, right?

Since it was already past 5:30 by the time I got unloaded in Coupeville, I knew that I was going to be lucky to make it to the border at all today, but I was still determined to stop and smell the flowers on the way.

I took a short side trip to see the Admiralty Head Lighthouse. It's not as impressive as the Portland Head Lighthouse we saw last year in Maine, but it was still lovely.

Admiralty Head Lighthouse

This is actually the second lighthouse built to look out over Admiralty Inlet, but, like the first, it has been decommissioned now.

The lighthouse sits in Fort Casey State Park, which looks like a lovely place to sit and have a picnic if you're not five hours behind schedule. As I drove through the park, a small herd of deer wandered in front of me. They did not seem even slightly concerned that I might have a hankering for venison.

The first wildlife of the trip

I included the picture of these deer because they are the first wildlife I'd seen. I anticipated seeing much more as I crossed British Columbia and the Yukon territory. I was thinking of putting together a wildlife bingo card with all the possible animals I might see on this trip—moose, caribou, bald eagles, seals, otters, whales, bears, foxes, etc. Zoos are great, but I had a hankering to see them in the wild, armed only with my trusty Canon.

A word about the photographs contained in the book: I am not a professional photographer. I don't have one of those cameras with the lenses that are longer than Cyrano De

Bergerac's nose. I am strictly an amateur, but at the same time, whenever possible, I want to share with you what I've seen. I hope you enjoy them. They look best when viewed on a Kindle that is full color.

I took Highway 20 north and across Deception Pass, so-named because British Captain George Vancouver, who charted the western coast of North America on expeditions in the 1790s, said it deceived him into thinking that Whidby Island was not an island at all, but a peninsula. Of course, the Coast Salish people had been living in the area happily for thousands of years, but it is Capt. Vancouver's name, and the names that he gave to many features of the coast, that have stuck. If you ever have a chance to drive over the Deception Pass Bridge, stop at either end and take a look at it, because it is a stunning example of bridge architecture:

Deception Pass Bridge

A Lap Around Alaska

There was something so symmetrical and lovely about the construction of the bridge—like a steel spider web—that I stood and admired it, listening to the rushing of water far below, for several long, happy minutes. Then I remembered how late it was getting and that darkness wasn't that far away, stopped dawdling, and shot straight north to Canada.

Unfortunately, the last part of my Day One drive was on I-5. At least that late in the day, and that far north of Seattle, there was no traffic. It was a smooth ride to the border.

As I approached on I-5, a sign announced wait times to cross the border. The crossing at Blaine—the most popular crossing—had a thirty-minute wait time. If you didn't mind getting off the interstate and taking a different crossing, the wait time was only five minutes. I am always happy to get off the interstate and did so.

Small confession time. I didn't really have the proper paperwork to cross the border. I should have had either a passport or an enhanced driver's license. I didn't have a passport, and I only *kind* of had an enhanced license. This trip came together very suddenly, but with the imminent birth of a grandbaby at the end of May, I didn't want to put off my departure any more than I had to.

So, I jumped through the necessary hoops to get the enhanced license. I was given a paper version and told that the permanent one would arrive in 10 to 14 days. I'd been checking the mail religiously every day since, but no license had appeared. The problem was, the temporary enhanced license I'd been given said specifically that it was not sufficient for crossing borders.

The day I left, I checked the mail on the way out of town, but still no license. I decided to just leave and count on my diplomatic skills and the fact that I actually am a U.S. citizen to get me across the border. Four times. I am an optimist!

As I pulled up to the Canadian border and saw the stern-faced border service agent, I immediately felt less optimistic. He curtly held his hand out and said, "Passport."

"Well ..." I said, and I could see that he didn't really want to hear whatever story I had to tell. He glanced at my paper license, my old photo license, and the certified birth certificate I had brought along.

"What are you going to be doing in Canada?" he asked.

"Writing a travel book."

He looked skeptical, but he had looked that way since I pulled up. To help my cause, I pulled out a copy of *A Lap Around America* and pointed to my name on the cover. He remained unimpressed. Obviously, my "fame" had not reached this far-flung location. To be honest, my fame rarely reaches the living room where Dawn sits while I write.

He handed my paperwork back and pointed to an empty parking lane next to a building. "Park there. Go inside. Present your paperwork at the desk. We'll see what they decide to do with you."

I can't say I liked the sound of that, as it appeared to be very open-ended. What were the options? Medieval torture chamber? Forcing me to listen to Justin Bieber or Bryan Adams albums for 24 hours as penance for not having my paperwork lined up? I would prefer the rack to the Bieber, please.

The inside of the building looked a lot like an airport terminal. I approached the desk, handed my paperwork in, and answered the same set of questions I had outside.

"Have a seat," the man said. "We'll call you back up."

I sat down beside two ladies who looked very comfortable, as if they might have been sitting there a long time. One was knitting. "Been here long?" I inquired.

"Oh, not too bad," the knitter responded without taking her

eyes off her work. "I started this," she said, nodding to the half-finished scarf, "after I got here."

I know I looked crestfallen, as I envisioned spending the first night of my road trip in the loving arms of Canadian customs.

She chuckled. "Just kidding. It's only been about an hour."

Eeesh. After spending five hours waiting for the ferry in Port Townsend, this might be the least-productive first day of a road trip ever. I thumbed my phone on. If I was going to be here for a while, I might as well get caught up on the news and social media. No dice. My cell had absolutely zero signal. So, I sat and waited. I wished I knew how to knit.

The wait was short, though, and just a few minutes later, I was paged to the counter.

The same man pushed my paperwork back to me. "You're good to go."

Younger, smart-aleck me would have made a wiseass comment that might have led to a longer stay with Canadian customs. Older, at least moderately wiser, me just said, "Thank you very much," and headed to the Emerald Bullet.

I pulled away from Customs slightly exhilarated, knowing that I had jumped one major hurdle, but feeling a little lost. I didn't have a British Columbia map, and since I hadn't gone through the main entry point, I really didn't know where I was. Typically, that's not a problem, but with my trusty Android phone still showing absolutely zero bars of Internet, I couldn't use Mama Google to figure out where I was.

I stopped at the first gas station and asked the bearded man behind the counter if he had a map of British Columbia. Canadians in general, and British Columbians in particular, are unfailingly polite and friendly. He smiled, laughed at the idea that someone would come to a gas station looking for a map in 2017, and shook his head. I should have known. On my trip around

America last year, I found that fewer than half of gas stations even carry paper maps any more.

"But where are you trying to go? I can help you." Unfailingly kind, as I said. "Alaska, ultimately, but heading toward Dawson Creek first, so I can catch the AlCan."

He nodded wisely, as though lost strangers wandered in every few hours looking for directions to the Alaska Highway. He rattled off a long list of directions that I immediately forgot. I walked out of the station mumbling, "Turn right at the next light," the first and only part of the complex directions that had stuck with me.

By then, it was almost dark. The truth is, I don't see that well after dark. Well enough that I feel comfortable driving around familiar ground, perhaps. But, lost in a strange country? Not ideal.

Soon enough, I found myself in a nice little town called Langley. It seemed filled with strip malls and box stores that I'm sure I would have recognized if I were Canadian. I pulled into one of these parking lots and spent fifteen minutes trying to figure out why my cellphone wasn't functioning as anything but a phone—so very twentieth century. I couldn't figure it out, but at least the phone itself worked, so I called Dawn and commiserated with her.

Dawn proved to be a valuable mission control for the road trip. While I sat in a dark corner of a rapidly emptying parking lot, she got in touch with our cell provider and tried to solve the problem of my missing Internet.

I had planned on spending a night or two in the car on the trip, but I wasn't really planning on it for the very first night. Nonetheless, I drove around the various stores until I found what looked to be a quiet little spot where I could spend the night if need be. I wake early anyway, so if I knew that if I had to sleep in an uncomfortable car seat, I would be up and around before anyone would come to find some strange American sleeping in their lot.

While I dug out my pillow and blanket, Dawn worked her magic. She called and relayed specific instructions to activate my service in Canada. I followed the steps exactly. Nothing. Still no service. I undid all the instructions, changed it back to the original settings, then walked through the whole process again.

Like magic, the phone began binging and bonging, delivering notifications from several pent-up hours. I called Dawn to thank her for rescuing me, told her it was for this very purpose that I had married her, then found an inexpensive motel nearby. Gotta love the Internet.

By 11 p.m., I was checked in and safely tucked in a bed much more comfortable than the front seat of a 1997 Subaru Outback.

Day Two

Waking up in Canada made me feel like the road trip was truly underway, even though I really wasn't that far from home yet. I felt a bit like a stranger in a strange land, though. First, there are the television stations. When I turned on a sports network, as I am wont to do, they were playing *Sportscenter*. Except it wasn't. It was *Sportscentre*. After I watched *Sportscentre* for about twenty minutes as I packed and prepared for the day, I realized they were only going to show hockey highlights. I've never been a hockey fan, so wall-to-wall coverage of hockey kind of sails over my head. I switched over to the History Channel and found one of my favorite shows: *American Pickers*. Except it wasn't. It was *Canadian Pickers*. Same basic concept—two guys traveling around the countryside, looking for rusty gold—but it wasn't Mike and Frank; it was two guys I didn't recognize. They did have awesome Canadian accents, though.

If you were to look at British Columbia from space, the route from Vancouver to Alaska would be obvious—just head north and slightly west, and you'll get there. The reality is much different. Not unlike Alaska, there are large portions of British Columbia and Yukon that have no roads at all. In short, there are no roads that run directly north-south. Even if there were, that would mean I would miss driving the Alaska Highway, which I assumed would be one of the high points of the trip.

The Alaska Highway starts in Dawson Creek, British Columbia. The distance from Langley to Dawson Creek is 715 miles, so I knew I wouldn't make it to the beginning of the AlCan on this day. That was fine with me, as I was looking forward to seeing parts of British Columbia almost as much as I was getting to Alaska.

Before I left Langley, I decided to gas up. That's when I realized I was going to have to do way more math than I am used to. Since America stubbornly rejected the metric system back in the '70s, I had never learned how much a liter (or *litre*) really was, or how far a kilometer is. I spent much of my mental energy on this day converting things into numbers I could relate to.

Let's start with distance. A kilometer is .62 of a mile. That's a little difficult for my feeble mind to do on the fly, so I figure it at two-thirds of a mile and then take a bit off. It's not exact, but when I'm just trying to find out how far away the next bathroom stop is, it doesn't have to be exact. Until it does, God forbid.

Even pumping gas requires figuring things out. When I arrived at the filling station, gas was $1.16 per liter. Is that expensive gas or not? Each liter is approximately one-quarter gallon. So, that comes out to $4.64 per gallon. Holy cow, that's a lot more than what I pay at home. But, wait, there's more math. I have to take the exchange rate into account. Today's exchange rate showed that each Canadian dollar only cost me $0.75 U.S. That comes out to about $3.50 per gallon. Still higher than I had been paying at home, where I'd filled up for $2.79 the day before, but not exorbitant.

Leaving Langley, I was forced to drive Highway 1, the Trans-Canada Highway. It's actually a freeway on that section, but I had no option, and I took comfort in the fact that, very soon, all freeways would be in my rearview mirror.

It was an absolutely gorgeous drive out of Langley toward Chilliwack. Does that name ring any bells for you? It does for me, but I was a disc jockey when the song, "My Girl (Gone,

Gone, Gone)" by the band Chilliwack was a hit back in 1981. It was a catchy tune, so I ended up playing it several hundred times on the radio, because that's what disc jockeys do, right? We find songs we kind of like and then play them until the listeners are sick of them. In any case, I was happy to drive through the little town of Chilliwack, where the band did indeed originate back in the early '80s.

Chilliwack felt like a farming area, with huge, verdant green fields that stretched to the horizon. Before long, though, Highway 1 climbed a bit, and I found myself surrounded by the fog-shrouded Cascade Mountains on one side and the Fraser River on the other.

The Cascades along Highway 1

I spent a lot of time running alongside the Fraser River this day, which is not surprising. The Fraser is over 800 miles long, the longest river in British Columbia. It has a bit of an odd color, or at least it did on this day—a bit like coffee with creamer added, but just a hint of green. It sounds unappealing, but really, it is a picturesque river.

The Fraser River

When I stopped to take that picture I noticed how incredibly good the air smelled. I live at the southwestern tip of Washington, about 100 yards from the Pacific Ocean. Our little town has very clean, sea-scented air. Still, there was something about breathing in this brisk British Columbia air that was special. Each breath was almost like taking a bite from a crisp apple.

After heading east on Highway 1 for over an hour, I came to Hope, British Columbia, where I turned north. After driving due east for the entire morning, when my ultimate goal was to go north and west, it finally felt as though I was making some progress toward my ultimate goal.

I've mentioned what I call "happy accidents" before. I love it when something reaches out and surprises me. That happened just before lunchtime on Day Two. I had pulled off the road to get something to drink out of the cooler. Every time I wanted to grab a water or juice, I had to pull off the road because Dawn had made me promise to keep the cooler in the back of the Emerald Bullet so that I wouldn't be tempted to try to fish a water or pop out while driving. I dutifully pulled off the road and looked down into a little ravine, only to see this:

An unexpected opportunity

An amazing little cemetery down the hill. I would never have seen if I hadn't pulled off the road in that exact spot. It's a mixture of old and new graves, although the oldest only seemed to date back 100 years or so. After seeing graves from the 1700s in Salem, Massachusetts, last year, I am tougher to impress. Still, as always, I found headstones that tugged at my heart:

So much heartache in one picture

I continued on north through tiny towns like Hells Gate, Keefers, and Kanaka Bar. Truth be told, these are more like wide spots in the road than actual towns. Eventually, I came to a fork in the road where I needed to either veer right to stay on Highway 1, or stay the course and get on Highway 12. Ultimately, it didn't matter much, because both highways eventually meet up again farther north, so I flipped a mental coin and decided to stay with Highway 1.

I was glad I did, as that took me through Spences Bridge. Please note that this is not a typo, though it makes my fingers itch to type it that way. Wouldn't "Spence's Bridge" feel a little better? In any case, there is no apostrophe, just as in Harpers Ferry, West Virginia. Honestly, I was planning on bypassing Spences Bridge and driving on to Ashcroft or Boston Flats before stopping for lunch, but I saw an interesting building off to the side of the road, the kind of thing that will always make me pull over.

Church? Residence? No idea.

If you read *A Lap Around America*, you know that old, semi-deserted buildings are hopelessly alluring to me. This one was obviously not deserted, but it was so interesting, I sat and stared at it for a few minutes. If anyone was home and saw me stalking them, at least they didn't come out on the front porch with a shotgun loaded with rock salt. I don't know if this was once a church, but the steeple sure seems to indicate that. Now it appeared to be living quarters for someone. To me, the weathered shingles, combined with the bell-less steeple and the tiny size, fascinated me.

Once I was off the road, I thought I might as well grab a bite. A few blocks past the old church building, I found a restaurant called The Packing House, so named because the building had once been used for packing apples. I love a place with a bit of history, and The Packing House filled the bill. It was a bit odd-looking, with a fenced-in, mostly dirt area in front of the

A Lap Around Alaska

restaurant, with a few tables scattered about. Since the temperatures were in the upper 40s at the moment, I opted for inside dining.

As soon as I walked in, I had the feeling I was the only person in the place that didn't know every other person in the place. There were four older women having lunch together, another table of working men, and various couples around the room. Conversations were not limited to table companions—everyone seemed to be conversing with everyone else. I sat a bit off from everyone, feeling like a lump on a log.

The waitress was friendly and the BLT was good, though. The waitress filled me in a bit on the history of the place. She said it was a "prefab" house that had been delivered across the Atlantic Ocean and put together here in B.C. over a hundred years before. It did have a very solid feel to it, as did all my fellow diners. I managed to eavesdrop on a lot of conversations filled with local gossip and predictions about the hockey playoffs, but noticed that I didn't see a single iPhone or Android in evidence. People were just talking to each other. It was nice. I felt like I had stepped back in time about thirty years or so.

A few miles north of Spences Bridge, Highway 1 diverged to the east and I stayed on a steady north progression via Highway 97. The farther north I drove, the more I noticed the lakes. Small lakes, long lakes, wide lakes—it felt as though there were bodies of water everywhere. Toward the end of the day, I saw the first lake that was still frozen over. Its little post-winter breakup was still in progress, with ribbons of open water running through the ice. I knew that, as the trip progressed, I would see much more ice than open water.

When I hit the road this morning, I had dreams of making it to Prince George, but between getting a late start and then pulling off to the side of the road several dozen times to gawk at the scenery, I just didn't make it. It was one of my goals for the trip not to drive much after dark. Luckily, the farther north I drove, the later it would get dark.

I gave up for the day when I got to Quesnel, a decent-sized town. Eventually, I located a pretty terrible little motel right next to an operating paper mill. It looked industrial and ugly—exactly what I was looking for on this trip. If you're wondering, there were much nicer hotels and motels in Quesnel, but they were $30 or so more for the night. When I know that all I am going to do is sleep for six or seven hours, I'll always take the cheaper option. All of which may explain, once again, why Dawn didn't want to come with me.

Day Three

"Oooh, if you have never been to Alaska, go there while it is still wild. My favorite uncle asked me if I wanted to go there, Uncle Sam. He said if you don't go, you're going to jail. That is how Uncle Sam asks you." —**Bob Ross**

I got an early start this day. My eyes flew wide open at 4:30 a.m., and that was that—I was awake for the day. Maybe it was all the pent-up excitement of knowing that I was finally about to reach the Alaska Highway. That was where this road trip would really begin.

Whereas southern British Columbia is truly beautiful, the central and northern sections of the province I drove through on this day are somewhat less so. The mountains, rivers, and deep greens seemed to devolve into hills covered with scrub and lots of grays and browns.

That meant I made a little better time in the morning, though, as there weren't so many spots that tempted me to pull off to the side of the road, sit on the hood of the Emerald Bullet, and just gaze out over the landscape as if I was the first human to ever see it.

The early start, combined with the steadier driving pace, meant that I was able to cover the 350 or so miles between Quesnel and Dawson Creek by early afternoon. Please note I said "Dawson Creek," as opposed to *Dawson's Creek*, the angst-ridden 1990s television show. I stopped in a little café for lunch and to regroup. All my plans had pointed to getting me this far, so what was next?

Next, of course, was the AlCan. Since Dawson Creek is Mile 0 of the Alaska Highway, this is probably a good spot to talk about the road. The Alaska Highway was constructed during World War II. There were actual battles fought with the Japanese on Alaskan soil during that war, so there was a logical need to be able to transport goods and men from the Lower 48 directly to Alaska without loading and unloading a ship. The Alaska Highway was the answer.

Since it was built as a basic transportation road, it was indeed basic. People who drove the AlCan in the early days took their lives into their own hands. There's no comparison between those days and what you'll encounter as you drive it now.

The first time I became aware of the AlCan was in the 1970s. Back then, people who had driven it wore that achievement as a badge of honor, like being in the front lines in battle. "You should see the potholes," people would say. "They're so deep, if you fall in one, you end up in China." There was a lot of talk about broken axles and people who felt fortunate to escape with their lives. I expected to see a lot fewer potholes big enough to hide a Winnebago in now than I would have back then.

Initially, the AlCan was 1,700 miles from beginning to end, but constant road construction that rerouted and straightened it out has lopped off more than 300 miles of that distance. Still, even with the improved roads and the shortened distance, driving the AlCan is an adventure, and one that shouldn't be approached lightly.

There are stretches of hundreds of miles where there is absolutely no sign of civilization, not to mention no cell towers. If you break down or have an accident in the wrong spot, you can sometimes wait quite some time before someone else comes along, and there is no nearby tow truck or garage. This is why I replaced every belt and hose that had any wear and put four brand new shoes on the Emerald

Bullet.

Just a few miles outside Dawson Creek, I saw my first sign for the Alaska Highway, which felt momentous.

Finally!

Right at that sign, I noticed there was also a loop off the main road. I like loops. You often get the chance to see something you wouldn't see otherwise, so I turned off the Alaska Highway almost as soon as I had gotten on it.

It was well worth it. A few miles down the loop, I came to the historic Kiskatinaw Bridge, also known as the Old Curved Bridge. If you make this drive, I really recommend taking the first loop to the north, about twenty miles outside of Dawson Creek, because the Old Curved Bridge is worth the price of admission. (Which is free, so maybe that's not a good analogy.)

The Kiskatinaw Bridge

The bridge was celebrating its seventy-fifth anniversary in 2017, hence the "old" part of its nickname. In addition to being old, though, there's that curve, as seen in the photo above. It was built to replace a temporary bridge built by the U.S. military when the road was first constructed. From north to south, the bridge curves nine degrees, which was made necessary by the geography on each side of the abyss it spans.

Just driving over the aged, wooden planks, feeling the curve of the bridge, was a nice experience. Of course, I stopped on one side and walked out on it. As I did, a car came from the other direction. I tensed a bit, not sure exactly how stable it was. I felt the tires hit the wood all right, but it held up pretty good for seventy-five years old.

The beauty of the curved bridge is matched by its underpinnings. I wanted to walk down to the base and get a picture looking up at the bridge, but with snow on the ground, I had a terrible feeling I would be down there until it melted. So, I settled for this picture from the slope above. A reader of my blog who lives in Dawson Creek told me that the underside of the Old Curved Bridge used to be quite the party spot back in the day.

Party spot: Old Alaska Highway version

One thing I learned on my first small leg on the AlCan was that places that appear on maps to be towns really aren't towns at all. If you're lucky, there is a gas station there. Maybe a café, but beyond that, nada. I was keeping a full gas can in the back of the Emerald Bullet, but even so, I made a mental note to fill up at every opportunity.

I made it to Pink Mountain before I stopped for the night. Why is it called Pink Mountain? When I asked at the Buffalo Inn, where I stayed, they said a nearby mountain had pinkish rocks in it. I couldn't see any pink rocks—only snow and mud. One thing I was learning is that in springtime on the Alaska Highway, mud is everywhere. There isn't a lot of pavement beyond the road itself, and the melting snow and heavy rains mix with the good Canadian soil to make a wonderful muck of everything. The Buffalo Inn, like many places on the highway, had big metal grates in its approach, so I had a chance to knock the majority of the brown, gooey stuff off my shoes.

I probably could have pushed on a bit farther for the day, but towns are few and far between. It was a good day. Almost 450 more miles under my wheels, and now firmly on my journey.

Day Four

So, if you've ever wondered what the weather is like in the foothills of northern British Columbia in late April, I can tell you. It's chilly. When I woke up in the morning, the first thing I did was thumb my phone awake and check the weather. When I did that on this day, it said the temperature was 22 degrees, with possible snow flurries in the forecast. It looked like I might have one last chance to feel winter before spring fully arrived.

I pulled my handy *Milepost* map of the AlCan out and checked the road ahead. It looked like a lot of rise and fall in elevation, including the highest point on the AlCan: Summit Pass. I filled up in Pink Mountain, based on the idea that you get gas at every opportunity on the way. Even so, I was down to about a quarter of a tank before I saw the next sign of civilization. I was concerned I might have to use the two and a half gallons in the gas can, but I was saved from that.

On this day, I really didn't see any towns at all. Instead, there were what might be called "stops." As in, a place in the middle of nowhere where you can stop and get gas and something to drink. I love to stop for a few minutes and chat with the people that operate these small businesses. I can only imagine what it's like to live so far from civilization that if you don't have something, you just do without it. I talked to any number of proprietors of this kind of store/restaurant/gas station, and I learned something important. Every one of them, without exception, gave off a calm, happy air. They smiled, laughed, answered all my inane questions—"What happens if you run out of bread?" Answer: "We bake more"—and struck me as very settled on their decision to live apart from the world.

I didn't know how far it might be between gas stations on this deserted stretch of highway, so I filled up at every opportunity—even if I still had three-quarters of a tank. I paid around $5 a gallon when I filled up in Pink Mountain, but honestly, I was surprised it wasn't more. They've kind of got you where they want you. If it had been $10 per gallon, what else was I gonna do? Strap a hundred-gallon gas tank to the roof of the Subaru? I was quite happy to pay $5 or $6 a gallon.

In any case, I got on the road by 6:30 a.m., and from then until mid-afternoon, I drove on snow, ice, or slush, take your pick. They've all got their downsides. The temperatures never rose out of the low 20s, which meant that the slush that flew up from the tires slowly built up on the sides of the Subaru. After fifty miles or so, it looked like it had been painted brown and had gained a few hundred pounds.

The roads were fairly treacherous through this stretch, but this is where the all-wheel drive of the Outback came in handy. As long as I kept my speed down, which I did, I never had any trouble. Not sure I would have wanted to tackle it in a rear-wheel-drive minivan, though.

Here's a pretty typical shot of what I saw beside me throughout the morning:

Yes, it is still a bit chilly in April

I was beginning to feel a little disappointed that I hadn't seen any wildlife yet. Then, animals started to pop up everywhere. The first sighting of the day was two caribou. They were understandably skittish and didn't want to hold still and pose for a picture, but I did manage to snag a picture of one as it trotted away from me.

My first Canadian wildlife

I drove alongside Muncho Lake for quite a few miles. I'm sure it's beautiful in summer, when it is full of clear blue water, but today it looked a lot like this:

A snow- and ice-covered Muncho Lake

When I had announced on my writer's Facebook page that I was going to drive the AlCan, several people told me to be sure to stop at Liard Hot Springs. Liard is the second largest hot springs in Canada and has two pools that range in temperature from 108 degrees to 125 degrees. Think of a hot tub on steroids. There's a nice boardwalk that runs right out to the hot springs, and it all sits right on the Alaska Highway.

I saw the sign on the right and turned into Liard Hot Springs Provincial Park. And ... found absolutely nothing. There was a foot of snow on the ground, and the small welcome shack was completely deserted. I glanced in my rearview mirror. I saw one set of tire tracks—mine. I thought a hot spring would be great in the cold and snow, but it didn't look like anyone else agreed with me. Liard Hot Springs was a ghost town. Slightly bummed out, I turned around and got back on the highway.

Eventually, the road dropped down in elevation, both the weather and the road cleared, and I managed to grip the steering wheel not quite so tightly. There were flurries off and on for the rest of the day, but the road stayed clear.

Then, the bison began to appear. For the rest of the day, they were as common as seeing a dairy herd while driving through rural Western Washington. I started counting how many of them I saw, but gave up when I hit triple digits. The fact that there were so many didn't detract from how cool it was to see them in the wild, grazing contentedly.

Not sure he likes the looks of me

Nothing will drive home the realization that you are on an adventure like seeing a small herd of bison grazing alongside the highway as though it's no big deal.

Oh, just a herd of a couple of dozen bison

Between the bison and the caribou, I was having a pretty good day. But it got even better. On a long, straight stretch, I saw another car sitting on the right side of the road. There are so few cars on the highway in April that meeting one is something of an event. The fact the driver had pulled off might mean the occupants needed help, or that they'd spotted something cool.

I pulled in front of them and shouted back, "You okay? Need help?" They pointed to a field to the south in silent reply. I followed their direction and saw a gorgeous red fox. He wasn't shy, and he wasn't in a hurry. He casually walked around in circles, sat for a while to pose, then walked a bit more. He was so photogenic I thought I might be witnessing a supermodel among foxes.

The Fabio of foxes

I watched him circling and moving for ten or fifteen minutes. The occupants of the car who had originally spotted him passed on with a wave, but I couldn't think of a single reason to leave. When would I again have a chance to watch a fox in the wild? Eventually I noticed that his circling and jogging was moving him closer and closer to my location. Something about the way he was staring made me look over my shoulder, where I saw this:

Check out the length of her tail

While I was focusing on the second fox, the first crossed the road behind me and quickly made his way toward her. They ran off up a hill together. Maybe I had just witnessed the fox equivalent of a blind date. One thing was for sure—it was an exhilarating experience, watching them gambol and frolic in the wild.

It had been an interesting day, starting off with climbing up and down various mountain passes, driving over snow and ice for hours at a stretch, then wandering into a Disneyland of wild critters. When I had been ensconced in my snug little house in Seaview, Washington, last winter, dreaming of this trip, this was exactly the kind of day I was hoping for.

By dinnertime, I crossed out of British Columbia and into Yukon. One more milestone reached. I stopped for the night in Watson Lake, Yukon. A quick word about finding lodging on the Alaska Highway. Real towns are few and far between, so you might have to stop a little earlier than you'd prefer, or risk driving a lot longer than you had planned. For instance, after Watson Lake, there was no other town with lodging for more than two hundred miles.

I had been on the road for thirteen hours and my odometer showed that I had covered more than 450 miles of the Alaska Highway on that first full day on it. That was good enough. Doing the math, I saw that I'd averaged 35 miles for each hour I was on the road. Of course, that takes into account more than a dozen stops to absorb the scenery or watch wildlife.

I settled in for the night at a place called the Big Horn Motel in Watson Lake. One of the things I always verified before I booked a room was that they had real, functioning wi-fi. Not so much for Internet surfing purposes—by the end of a day of driving, I was usually ready to collapse into bed early—but to make sure that I would be able to upload my photos for the day onto my blog. A few hundred people followed the blog, and I hated to miss a day in posting to it.

When I checked in, I asked the desk clerk if I needed a password for Internet access. He nodded and took a slip of paper out of a drawer. There was a password and username scrawled across it.

"It's good for limited use."

"I just want to upload my pictures to my blog."

"Oh, yes, no problem, no problem."

I went to my room and set my bags in the bathtub so I could do my nightly bedbug check. This was a handy travel tip I'd picked up on our Lap Around America last summer. Most people set their bags on their bed when they walk into the room. If, however, the room has bedbugs, even if you spot them on an initial check, it's likely you'll take them with you wherever you go, courtesy of your suitcase. Instead, it's a good idea to set your bags somewhere safe—the porcelain of a shower or tub works nicely—while you conduct your bedbug search. You don't have to be fanatical about it, but I do always pull back the sheets at the corner of the bed to look for the nasty little critters.

Having verified that the room was bedbug-free, I set my laptop up on the little table in the corner. I uploaded two of the eight or so pictures I wanted for the blog that night, and a notification flashed on my screen that I had used all the Internet available for the day.

I walked back down the hall to the front desk and told the clerk what had happened. He fixed me with a conspiratorial look, then said, very loudly, "You're watching porn, aren't you?"

It was so surreal, it made me laugh out loud.

"No, I'm just trying to upload my pictures to my blog, like I told you."

He shook his head and said again, as if there could be no doubt, "You're watching porn."

The whole scenario was starting to lose its limited charm.

For a third time, I confirmed I just wanted to get my blog updated so I could go to bed.

He nodded, reached into the drawer and took out three more of the pieces of paper with different codes written on them and slid them across the desk. As I reached for them, he gave me a sly wink, as if we shared a secret.

I just sighed, went back to the room and finished uploading my pictures.

Overall, I was pleasantly surprised by the cost of the roadside motels along the Alaska Highway. Once I took the Canadian exchange rate into account, I was able to find a decent place in Watson Lake for about $75, and that was typical of the journey. Please don't misunderstand—the places that I stayed were not lovely. To call them "basic" would be to give them a considerable upgrade. Still, I was able to find safe, clean, warm lodging on the AlCan, as long as I planned ahead a bit.

Day Five

Somehow, my body's circadian rhythm had been thrown off. I was in the same time zone as my home, so that wasn't the problem. I think it might have been the fact the sky brightens so early in Yukon in spring, and gets dark so late. This morning, I noticed that there was light a little after 4 a.m. I was rarely staying up late enough to see what time it got dark.

Whatever the case, I was awake and stumbling around by 4:30 a.m. That gave me time to have a quick breakfast in the café attached to the hotel and still be on the road by 6:30. Typically, I don't eat breakfast in a restaurant, but looking at the map, I saw there was a long stretch of open road ahead of me and not many towns, so I fueled myself and the car alike before I left.

I made one early-morning stop on the way out of Watson Lake, at one of the most famous tourist attractions on the Alaska Highway—the Sign Post Forest. The Sign Post Forest is like a perfect piece of Americana, though it happens to be located in Canada. The whole thing started innocently enough, back when the Alaska Highway was being constructed. U.S. Army Private Lindley was ordered by his commanding officer to fix a sign that had been knocked over while the road was being worked on. He did, but in a flash of genius, he added a new sign that pointed toward his hometown, Danville, Illinois, along with the distance. He had no idea what he had started. Ever since, people have been adding their own signs to Private Lindley's creation. The site now covers several acres and has more than 77,000 signs, with more being added every day.

The kitschiest spot on the Alaska Highway

People have posted beautiful, hand-carved signs, or simple handmade ones that commemorate their own epic road trip. I saw one that read, "Puerto Panesco, Mexico, to Talkeetna, Alaska." Some reflect a life philosophy, like the one that read, "Who needs a man when you have a dog?" with two massive paw prints beneath it. Who can argue with that? Some are sentimental, like the one that read, "We traveled 2,044 kilometers to see these beautiful, wonderful, quirky, amazing people be blessed in marriage," along with the name of the lucky couple.

The Sign Post Forest is open 24 hours a day, although it's best seen in daylight, as there doesn't appear to be any lighting. There is no admission fee and no formal structure. It's on the right side of the road just as you leave Watson Lake heading north. I recommend you take an hour or two, because there are a million stories to be discovered there.

The weather was better today. A bit warmer, too, with temperatures in the mid-30s. There were a few times, at higher elevations, when I saw a few snow flurries, but overall, there was plenty of blue sky and sunshine, too.

I'd been away from home almost a week now. Do I get lonely, driving so far all alone? I really don't. Like almost any writer, there's a lot going on between my ears. How can I be lonely when I have so many people who live inside my head? Plus, I have a lot of ways to pass the time—I brought some great music, I plot out the books I'm going to write when I get home, I am constantly scanning for wildlife, and I listen to audiobooks. Today, I spent most of the day on the road listening to the audio version of Ken Follett's *Pillars of the Earth*. *Pillars* is more than 30 hours long, so it's made for a road trip like this.

I missed Dawn, and knew this trip would be so much better if she were with me. But aside from that, I was really content traveling alone. Just after noon, I pulled over to eat a sandwich from the Magical Mystery Bag and sat staring at a frozen lake for fifteen minutes. Not a single car passed in either direction. That's when it hit home just how *alone* I really was.

I've also found that while I am on the road, I am essentially cut off from the 24-hour news cycle we live in most of our lives. I was sure scandals were happening, some athlete did or said something stupid, and Kim Kardashian was wearing a new hairstyle, but out there, it all feels far away—not just in distance, but in perspective. When I called Dawn to catch up, she'd ask, "Did you see ..." this or that. The answer, quite happily, was always no. I don't know if we realize how hardwired we are into this kind of information until we find ourselves almost completely cut off. Each little motel I stayed at had a television, but after the first night on the road, I don't think I bothered to turn it on. It's pretty nice being cut off from the twenty-first century.

Just before I got to Teslin, there was a wide pullout spot that looked out over the village of Teslin and the Nisutlin River Delta. It's a wonderful place to stop for the view and to rest for a bit.

The Nisutlin Bay Bridge

There is something you need to know about the rest areas along the AlCan. In the lower 48, rest areas range a lot in quality. For instance, Missouri tends to have clean, wonderful rest areas that are truly welcoming. Nevada, on the other hand, seems to use its rest areas as an entrance point to hell itself. On the AlCan, though, there isn't a lot of variety. They are all primitive. The best of them have a building, but none has running water. That means the toilets lean more toward the outhouse style than a flushable toilet. In fact, many of the "rest areas" are simply wide gravel areas where you can park and rest, with no facilities at all. A good safety tip is to bring along your own toilet paper, because I didn't see a single roll anywhere along the highway.

A typical AlCan rest area

As I stood in the rest area looking out over Teslin, a late-model pickup coming the other direction pulled in and stopped. An older couple got out to stretch their legs. I've found that most everyone who stops at rest areas, especially in Alaska and Yukon, is anxious to talk to someone else. We all have the road and the weather in common out there.

"Where you coming from?" the woman asked me.

"Down by Portland, Oregon," I answered. I usually don't bother trying to explain where Seaview is, so I settle on Portland as a landmark.

Two sets of eyebrows shot up, and they both laughed.

"Well, how about that? That's where we're heading! We're hoping to get there by Sunday night. Do you think we'll make it?"

I did a little calculating in my head. I didn't think so.

"Monday's a lot more likely, I'd say. I'm taking my time, but it's taken me four and a half days to get this far."

They looked a little downcast.

"Well, no real hurry, I guess," she said.

I eyed the trailer behind their pickup. The man followed my eyes, then said, "We're moving down there."

"From where?"

"Fairbanks area. We don't want to leave, but we've got to. Family."

I nodded. I could see that the move was not a happy one for them, so I didn't pry further. As I've mentioned, Alaskans are a special breed, and it can be hard on them when they have to go "outside," their word for the Lower 48. I felt bad for them, wished them luck on the remainder of their journey and drove across the bridge to Teslin.

Teslin is a cute, quaint little town, with an interesting museum that I wanted to check out, but it was closed. This is one of the downsides of driving the AlCan in April. Probably half of the small gas stations and small businesses that dot the highway were still closed down, waiting for the high season, which was at least a month away.

I hit Whitehorse by late afternoon. I was hungry and thinking about grabbing a bite to eat. There was a restaurant in the same building as the gas station where I fueled up, but it was a Chinese restaurant that looked a little forlorn. Somehow, a sad-looking little Chinese restaurant attached to a gas station in Yukon didn't inspire confidence in me. PB&J as I drove worked just fine.

I'd been seeing mountains on all sides every day since I got to British Columbia. As I approached the tiny town of Haines Junction, though, those mountains began to change. All the mountains I had seen to that point were lovely, with snow on the peaks and trees on the side. Suddenly, they became much more mountainous, with snow cascading all the way down the sides.

Boom. Mountains

Have you ever seen scenery so mindboggling, so *overwhelming,* that it brought tears to your eyes? It happened to me this day as I drove the last 20 kilometers into Haines Junction. It took my breath away. Alaska was still half a day's drive away, but I felt close, now.

Haines Junction looks like a decent-sized town on the map. Again, though, the reality is a little less. I was hoping to find a grocery store where I could restock my Magical Mystery Bag, but aside from a couple of gas stations with convenience-store food, there wasn't much available. Maybe I just missed it. I couldn't help but wonder, as remote as the town is, where do people go to get their groceries?

I pulled into the Glacier View Inn, another in my endless series of inexpensive little roadside motels on this trip, and went inside. The motel office is inside a small, dark bar that is attached to some of the rooms. As I was filling out the registration paperwork, I turned to a small gathering off to my right and asked, "So, if I have just one night in Haines Junction, is there anything I really need to do?"

That ground the conversation to a halt. They looked me up and down, then one of the ladies said, "Well, the hockey game's on in about an hour."

"Oh, thanks. I don't watch hockey, though."

Four chins simultaneously hit the table as they absorbed this information. They couldn't make the connection. I was standing right before them, big as life and obviously still breathing, but I didn't like hockey? Another lady nodded wisely and said, "Oh, wait. You're not Canadian, are you?"

I confirmed her intuition, and she said, "Then, the only thing to do in Haines Junction is get drunk. Cheers!" She drained the beer bottle in front of her.

Just then, a man came up beside me and asked for a case of beer. The barmaid/front desk clerk tilted her head at him and said, "Jimmy, the liquor store's open."

"I know, I know," he muttered, shuffling his feet. "I just don't want to go there."

"I'm gonna have to charge you a lot more than you'd pay at the liquor store."

"I know, I know."

I couldn't tear my eyes away from this human drama playing out in front of me. Why didn't Jimmy want to go to the liquor store? Was it run by his girlfriend, and he was in trouble with her? Had he gotten into a fight over the last bottle of Wild Turkey on the shelf the night before? Inquiring minds want to know.

"What did you do now so that you can't go in the liquor store?"

I really wanted to know the answer to that question, but my curiosity was not to be sated, as Jimmy just continued to stare down at his muddy boots.

The bar maid turned back into a front desk clerk and handed me my receipt and key. "104, hon, right in the corner."

I hated to leave the scene of so much human interest, but it had been another long day behind the wheel, and, finally, Alaska was in my immediate sights.

This little village sits at the edge of the single largest protected wilderness on Earth, made up of Kluane National Park and Reserve in Yukon, the Tatshenshini-Alsek Park in British Columbia, and, in Alaska, Wrangell-St. Elias National Park and Preserve and Glacier Bay National Park and Preserve. It is wild, untamed, and absolutely stunning.

I had dreamed of driving the AlCan for forty years. Now that I was near seeing that dream coming true, it was everything I had hoped it would be—and so much more. The solitude, the pristine air, the constant glimpses of wildlife, and the astounding scenery had already given me memories I will cherish forever.

Day Six

"To the lover of wilderness, Alaska is one of the most wonderful countries in the world." —John Muir

Haines Junction may be a tiny little town, but it features huge views. Here's a shot I took from right outside the front door of the little motel where I stayed.

View from Haines Junction, Yukon

I gassed up at the little station in the picture above and headed for Alaska. It had taken me almost a week on the road, but I knew I'd get there this day, God willing and the creek don't rise.

As I drove the AlCan, I was constantly scanning both sides of the road—looking for wildlife, of course, but also anything else unexpected. An hour or two north of Haines

Junction, I found that unexpected something: a scattering of unknown artifacts off to the right side of the road. Of course, I had to stop and investigate.

An AlCan roadside memorial

It turned out to be a memorial to a young man named Douglas Richard Twiss II, a.k.a. "Dougie." The memorial consists of various carvings, totems, and headstones that all have particular meaning. There's a bench where you can sit amid it all and contemplate the serenity of the surroundings.

At the bottom of a large headstone is this quote: "Follow your dreams, be kind, and always remember to enjoy every day of your life." There are many worse life philosophies than that. In fact, that lines up with my own ideas pretty closely.

The memorial was designed by Doug Twiss, the father of Douglas Twiss II. I thought it was an awfully cool way to channel sadness and grief over the loss of a child into something that looks like it will stand for many years.

While at the memorial, I took a shot of the Emerald Bullet against the bright blue Yukon sky, still pretty well covered with mud and muck.

The Emerald Bullet, slightly less emerald than when we started

Now that I was reaching the end of the AlCan Highway, I was already starting to feel a little nostalgic for it. I found myself pulling over at every rest stop, walking around, just absorbing the atmosphere. I stopped at one just before noon to eat lunch. It was a gorgeous, warm day, so I opened the car door and sat looking out at the scenery. As I did, a magpie started entertaining me. Or maybe trying to run me off, I can't be sure. In any case, I was entertained enough to throw the crust of my sandwich to it before I left.

A Lap Around Alaska

A magpie along the AlCan

By mid-afternoon, I finally made it to the U.S. border. As I pulled up, I wondered if it would be easier or more difficult to cross into America without all my paperwork properly lined up. I needn't have worried.

First, there was absolutely no line, so I pulled right up to the man in the booth, who I could tell was listening to an audiobook as he waited for the next vehicle. That got us off on the right foot, as I love to talk to people about books. We swapped info on what each of us was listening to, then I gave him the paperwork I had. He riffled through it, asked me a couple of questions, and said, "Have a nice day."

Just like that, I was back in Alaska for the first time since 1978. A hundred yards past the border, I saw a speed limit sign that was in miles per hour. What a relief. I could now forgo doing the math until I was on my way home.

This portion of Alaska looks a lot like the Yukon that I left behind, which is to say, beautiful. My first official stop in Alaska was in Tok. As I approached the town, I saw a swarm of runners and walkers participating in a 5K race. There were quite a few entrants for such a small place; Tok has a population of only 1,200. Either people came from all around, or Tokians are a very fit people.

It was still relatively early in the day, but almost a week of solid driving up British Columbia and across the AlCan had worn me out, so I pulled into the first motel I saw and checked in. I asked the desk clerk (this one was a combo hostess/desk clerk, a step up from the bartender/desk clerk I'd had the day before) how to pronounce "Tok." I was hoping it was pronounced "tock," as in "tick-tock." Not the case, though. It's pronounced "toke" like the old Brewer and Shipley song, "One Toke Over the Line."

I was still low on groceries, so I found an actual grocery store—the first I'd seen in several days. I remember that, when I was in Alaska back in the '70s, prices were quite a bit higher than at home. That hadn't changed. A normal-sized bag of Doritos chips, $2.79 at home, was $5.99 in Tok. Gulp. Doritos were definitely not going to be on the menu, which was probably a good thing for my cholesterol anyway. Everything in the store was priced 50 percent higher than I would have paid in Washington state. Maybe, I thought, it's just because Tok is remote and not on normal shipping lines. If so, I'd have to stock up when I got to Fairbanks or Anchorage.

Since I couldn't seem to shake the habit of waking up at 4:30 a.m., I hit the hay early my first night back in the 49th state, ready to begin exploring the next day.

Day Seven

"For sheer majestic geography and sublime scale, nothing beats Alaska and the Yukon." —Sam Abell

I'll admit it. I like kitsch. Americana. Roadside attractions. Two of the highlights of my Lap Around America were seeing "The Famous JFK's World's Largest Ball of Twine" in New York, and the Abita Mystery House in Louisiana. There's something so nostalgic, so warmhearted about an attraction that knows it's not glitzy, not technologically driven, not current, but that puts its best foot forward anyway, that it's irresistible to me.

Just a few miles west of Tok, I found Mukluk Land. I can't imagine I will find anything kitschier than Mukluk Land, and it's one of the best things I saw on this trip.

You had me at "giant mukluk"

Unfortunately, as you can see in the photo, Mukluk Land was still covered in snow when I passed by, which put me in a quandary. I was dying to get in and poke around, but only silence greeted my calls of, "Hello, anybody there?" What to do, what to do? Climb back in the Emerald Bullet and continue on my way like a sane person, or walk on into the park and have a look around?

I approached the perimeter of the park carefully. A single "No Trespassing" sign would have been enough to send me on my way, but there was none in evidence. I remembered the advice of the first man I talked to in Alaska: "Just assume that everyone's armed, and you'll be right more often than you're wrong," and called out another "Halloo!"

When only a soft echo answered me, I stepped forward toward the entrance to Mukluk Land. Immediately, I broke through the hard crust of the snow and sank down a foot. I glanced around. There were no footprints to be seen, man or animal. Apparently, no one had been here since the last snowfall.

I crunched my way into the park and was rewarded with a vista usually reserved for Golden Ticket visitors to Willy Wonka's Chocolate Factory. I'm sure that being in Mukluk Land is a unique experience at any time. After all, it bills itself as "Alaska's Most Unique Destination," and I'm not going to argue. It's unlike any theme or amusement park I've ever seen. It is a roadside attraction grown large, covering a few acres with its crazy hodgepodge of games, rides, memorabilia and artifacts.

One of the first things I saw was a hand-painted sign: "We made it to Alaska, but it wasn't easy." There were displays everywhere of things unkind people might call "junk," but which I preferred to think of as "Alaskana," a word I have just made up. There were giant machines, putt-putt golf, a building filled with thousands of dolls, the kind of signs designed for sticking your head through to pose for a funny picture, and even a souped-up Santa sled.

When you absolutely, positively have to deliver those toys tonight

Mukluk Land was founded thirty-two years ago by George and Beth Jacobs, and it is obviously a labor of love. I could have spent several hours wandering around Mukluk Land, but I was keenly aware that I was an uninvited guest, and I knew I had to take my leave. I would love to return someday when the sun is warm, the snow is gone, and children's laughter ripples through the park. I am sure it is a sight to behold.

Before lunch, I arrived in Delta Junction, the official end of the Alaska Highway.

The end of the road, officially

I was glad there was this small monument to mark the spot, to give me a sense of closure. Having reached the terminus of the Alaska Highway, here are some of my conclusions about driving the AlCan:

1. It's not nearly as bad as it used to be. The horror stories about washboard ruts and giant potholes are a thing of the past. I found less than ten miles of unpaved road over the entire distance, and even that wasn't too terrible if you slowed down to 40 mph or so.

2. Still, be prepared. It's not unusual to go more than 100 miles or more between any small sign of civilization, especially in October through April. It's important to have a good spare tire and a tool kit for small mechanical problems.

3. There's still bad weather in April. I spent half a day driving over ice, packed snow, and slush.

4. In mid-April, at least, traffic is very light. It wasn't unusual for me to drive twenty or thirty miles without seeing a vehicle in either direction. That means you should be prepared for a lot of solitude if you're traveling alone. I liked this part.

5. As far as I could tell, the Alaska Highway is litter-free. I don't recall seeing so much as a gum wrapper on the side of the road. It made me slightly more proud to be a human being than I normally am.

6. Be prepared to rough it. Many "rest areas" are just a wide spot on the side of the road where you can park and stretch your legs. Most have a garbage can. Many have primitive restroom facilities—emphasis on primitive. Picture a permanent porta-potty, and you're on the right track.

7. Most of the towns aren't much. They may look big on a map, but they're only big in comparison to the emptiness around them. If you're expecting to find a decent-sized grocery store, or a drugstore, or a "nice" hotel, you're probably going to be disappointed. I found that most of the towns I stopped in reminded me of traveling back in time—like to the '70s. Even the gas pumps are older, and most don't take credit cards at the pump.

8. There's lots of wildlife. I spent an entire day counting bison. My favorite sighting was the two photogenic foxes I watched get together over the course of half an hour. I saw caribou, hares by the dozen, two bald eagles, and more rodents than I could count, including one I rolled over at 65 mph but did not injure. I think he dropped a little chipmunk poop as I rocketed over him. I know I would have.

9. Driving the Alaska Highway was one of the best

things I've done in my lifetime. The solitude, the overarching beauty, and the impossibly sweet-smelling air together gave me the gift of a never-to-be forgotten experience. If you've always dreamed of driving the Alaska Highway, I encourage you to do so.

By the way, one thing you have to watch out for in Alaska is the mosquitos. They are a lot bigger than I remembered:

Notice the creative "Watch for wildlife" sign in the corner

I was pretty sure this would be the kitschiest day of the trip, what with Mukluk Land, giant mosquitos, and the North Pole. Wait. Check that. Not *the* North Pole, but North Pole, Alaska. The city of North Pole, Alaska, was so named in 1953, mostly to attract businesses, especially toy manufacturers. Can't you just see it? "Hey, kids, our toys come straight from the North Pole!"

I don't know how successful that strategy was, as the

town has a population only a shade over 2,000. The name change may not have attracted a lot of industry, but it did bring the big fella to town:

I already know which list I'm on, thank you

That is, according to local legend, the tallest Santa Claus in the world, standing 42 feet tall. The interesting thing to me is that it was originally built and installed in Westgate Mall in Seattle in 1968. I've been to that mall many times, including about that time, and I don't recall ever seeing it. You'd think I'd remember a 42-foot-tall Santa Claus.

In the same area as the very tall Santa is a reindeer farm and Santa's workshop, which I'm sure is a happenin' place in November and December. In April? Locked up tight.

Before I left North Pole, I saw something so amazing, I had to get on the phone and tell Dawn what I was seeing. She wouldn't believe me, so I took a picture to prove it to her.

Yes, children, these once dotted the landscape

Yep, a Blockbuster Video. Even more unusual, an open, functioning Blockbuster Video. I had to go inside and walk around. It was a bit like taking a trip back to the 1990s. It made me want to rent *Jurassic Park* on VHS, buy some microwave popcorn and find a VCR. Oddly enough, the vast majority of surviving Blockbuster stores are in Alaska, apparently because of the long, cold winter nights, and the lack of easily accessible high-speed wi-fi.

I knew nothing else was going to top my day of kitsch, so I drove on to Fairbanks, which, at 64 degrees, 50 minutes North—just 120 miles south of the Arctic Circle—was the farthest north I had ever been. I was always interested in visiting Fairbanks in the '70s, but my brother Mick told me, "Fairbanks is a city built on yellow snow." I don't know what he had against the city, as I found it quite nice.

Tomorrow, I would tackle the most dangerous drive of the entire trip, the road sometimes called "the loneliest highway in America," the Dalton Highway.

Day Eight

"If you're willing to travel, or just super-desperate, the best place in the world to meet unattached men is on the Alaska pipeline. I'm told that the trek through the frozen tundra is well worth the effect for any woman who wants to know what it feels like to be Victoria Principal." —Linda Sunshine

A brief history of the Alaska pipeline is in order, since it was my constant companion on this day's epic drive. It's sometimes called the Trans-Alaska Pipeline (TAP) or the Alyeska Pipeline, but folks in Alaska tend to simply call it "the pipeline."

I wasn't old enough to be driving yet when the first wave of the energy crisis hit us in 1973, but I remember it being a constant topic of conversation around my house. I remember my dad complaining that he was getting paid the same amount, but it was costing him a lot more to drive back and forth to his construction jobs.

The energy crisis led to a jump in oil and gas prices, which suddenly made exploring more remote oil-rich areas of the United States lucrative. That included Prudhoe Bay, well north of the Arctic Circle in Alaska. It took four years to build the pipeline, at least partially because of the hazards and difficulties that came with constructing something so massive in such harsh conditions. I was in high school while it was being built, but I have clear memories of young men in my town dreaming of and planning to go north to work on the pipeline. Tens of thousands of workers did, and for those years, Valdez (where the pipeline ended) and Fairbanks, the closest town to the construction, boomed.

In addition to the need to dig down into permafrost, construction of the pipeline was slowed by the fact that there were no roads between Fairbanks and Prudhoe Bay. Thus, the Dalton Highway was born. Technically called the James W. Dalton Highway, it's known to locals as the North Slope Haul Road, or, even more briefly, simply the Haul Road. Not for nothing was it featured on the very first episode of the television show *The World's Most Dangerous Roads*.

Of course, I wanted to drive it. Being a twenty-first century kind of guy, the first thing I did was a little research on the road—which in this case may not have been the best thing to do. By the time I was done with my research, I was pretty sure I was making a one-way trip through the outer circles of hell.

I found plenty of advice online. *Make sure you have two full-size spare tires before you go. You'll need them.* Or, *Take plenty of extra gas with you. If you break down, you'll need to keep your heater going so you don't freeze to death.* Or, *Be very careful what vehicle you take on the Dalton Highway. Four-wheel drive isn't legally required, but it should be.*

Okay.

I didn't have two full-size spare tires. In fact, I didn't have *one*. I had the tiny little spare that sits hidden in the back of the Subaru. I did check to make sure I had my jack, though, and I did have my can of gas in the back. Also, I had my Magical Mystery Bag, and I was sure that the Costco-sized bag of trail mix would stave off starvation for at least a week.

With some trepidation about what lay ahead, I checked out of my motel in Fairbanks by 6 a.m. and headed north.

The Dalton Highway doesn't start immediately once you leave Fairbanks. First, you have to drive north on Highway 2 for more than an hour, slowly leaving stores, coffee shops, and any other sign of civilization behind you.

Eventually, there is a turn-off for Highway 11—the Dalton Highway.

Welcome to the loneliest highway in America

Another piece of advice I read before starting off was that it is advisable to have sunglasses, because of the strain caused by the constant glare off snow. I rarely wear sunglasses, so I had stopped at a Walgreens in Fairbanks the previous night, where they were selling two pair for $20.

I put them on as I hit the Dalton Highway, then pulled off to take the picture above. I couldn't see anything through the sunglasses, though, so I set them on the roof while I took the picture. And promptly forgot about them. For those of you who read *A Lap Around America*, you might remember that I did the exact same thing with my wallet at the beginning of that road trip. I am not to be trusted with any item and the roof of my car.

About twenty miles down the road, I realized that the sun was indeed blinding me, reached for the sunglasses, and slapped my head like I was in a V-8 commercial. I knew it would take me at least 40 minutes to go back to look for them, so I made a mental note to check on the return trip. I was happy that the sunglasses had been two-for-twenty now, as the sun was exceptionally bright.

Once you're on the Dalton, it's not just civilization you've left behind—it's also pavement. The Dalton Highway is almost all gravel. Every once in a while, after jouncing along the rutted, rocky road for mile after mile, my tires hit smooth pavement for a short period of time. The quiet was deafening.

When I started out, I wasn't sure if I wanted to drive the whole length all the way to Prudhoe Bay or not. After about five miles of shaking bad enough to let me know I would need a chiropractic appointment in the near future, I decided against it. There are only two towns on the highway: Coldfoot, about halfway up, and Deadhorse, on the Arctic Sea. As charming and friendly as the town of Deadhorse sounded, I knew that would mean driving 500 miles of the roughest road imaginable today, then turning around tomorrow and doing the same trek again. It also meant a likely stay somewhere on the road behind the wheel of the car, bundled up against the chill. It might have been springtime in the rest of America, but north of the Arctic Circle, it still felt like winter.

So, Coldfoot it would be.

Since the Dalton Highway was built to transport

necessary goods for the Trans-Alaska Pipeline, it was built for semi traffic, and little thought was put into the finer things—like pavement, gas stations, or legitimate rest areas.

What you get instead are wide open vistas of northern Alaska and the pipeline itself, which is rarely out of sight.

The Dalton Highway

Take the road you see in that photo and multiply it by 400 more miles, and you'll have an idea of what it's like to drive the Dalton Highway. The only real change you experience driving it is a lot of variations in elevation as you go up and over various hills and through valleys. I averaged about 35 mph; the combination of loose gravel, corners, hills, and eighteen-wheelers makes for some pretty treacherous driving.

Because the weather had been clear for the previous few days, the road was very dry. So, when a semi barreled down on me, it sent up a huge rooster tail of dust, rocks, and dirt a hundred yards behind it, essentially blinding me for four or five seconds. I quickly learned to scope out the road ahead for curves and the like whenever I saw a semi coming.

After a few hours of driving, it was easy to ask myself why I had chosen to do this. I came up with a few answers. There's the old fallback—because it was there. More than that, though, I wanted to drive as much of Alaska as I could on this trip, and these few hundred miles of road beckoned. Finally, this might very well be my only chance to go north of the Arctic Circle, and I wanted to take it.

I was disappointed there were no dashes on the ground

What's the weather like at the Arctic Circle in late April? It's a little chilly. I had absolutely no cellphone signal the entire day, so I couldn't get a temperature reading, but I am resistant to cold. I can walk around in 20-degree weather in just my shirtsleeves for five or ten minutes before it starts to bother me. When I jumped out of the car to take the above picture, I was back inside grabbing my jacket within seconds. It was a beautiful day, with blue skies and not all that much wind, but it was still very chilly.

There are a few landmarks other than the Arctic Circle, too. At one point, I crossed a bridge over the Yukon River, still frozen of course.

The frozen Yukon River

There aren't many trees or bushes this far north. Anything that grows here has to survive long periods of darkness, snow, and incredible cold.

Because I got such an early jump on the day, I pulled into Coldfoot by mid-afternoon. On any other journey, you would pass by Coldfoot without so much as a backwards glance. Not on the Dalton, though. Coldfoot is the Paris of the Dalton Highway. Coldfoot boasts a population of about twenty, and doesn't look like much: a few industrial-type buildings and dwellings scattered around a vast wasteland of mud, albeit frozen mud.

However, it boasts two very vital things: a gas pump and the Trucker's Café. I was a little worried as I pulled up to the single gas pump. They could have charged me $25 a gallon and I would have had to pay it. I'll admit I would have calculated pretty carefully, though, so I would have coasted back into Fairbanks on fumes. Instead, it was a relatively reasonable $4.59 a gallon. I paid it gladly.

The Trucker's Café doesn't look like much on the outside. If I hadn't known it was going to be there, I very well might have missed it. And, that would have been too bad, because I enjoyed the place. The inside matches the outside—practical and no-nonsense. My waitress was a young woman in her twenties, who answered all my questions about living so far from civilization as though she hadn't been asked the same questions a million times.

She said she hadn't left Coldfoot in more than three months.

"Don't you get a little bit of island fever, being stuck in one tiny little place?" I asked.

A smile. "Yep."

"It took me more than six hours to get here from Fairbanks. Do you really have to drive that far just to get to town?"

"Nah. Company's got an airplane. They'll fly us down there every once in a while, when we're really goin' stir crazy."

Good enough. I had the BLT sandwich and fries, which were excellent. There is obviously no cellphone service in this remote area, but if you don't mind ponying up ten bucks, the Trucker's Café will sell you 30 minutes of Internet.

I returned to the Emerald Bullet, which was covered once again in road muck, and tried to decide what to do with the rest of my day. After being shaken to my bones for the first half of the day, I knew I didn't have what it took to push on to Deadhorse. Before I left Coldfoot, though, I wanted to make one stop.

I'd read a bit about the local cemetery. Since the town itself hadn't been around for too long, I knew there wouldn't be any old graves, but I wanted to see what a cemetery so remote looked like. I crossed the highway to the small settlement on the other side and found it.

The chilly and silent Coldfoot Cemetery

It was completely covered in three feet of frozen snow. Nothing to see but a snowbank inside the fence. I had my boots with me, but I didn't want to go tromping around over someone's grave when I couldn't see where I was walking. I guess if you want to see the Coldfoot Cemetery, you have to wait until later in the summer.

I said earlier that I had the pipeline to keep me company the entire drive, and that's true. Here's what it looks like as it runs parallel to the road.

The Trans-Alaska Pipeline

The pipeline wasn't my only company on the drive, though. Until I got far enough north that they began to peter out, there were hundreds of thousands of northern spruce trees along the road. Eventually, you do hit tundra, which means literally "treeless upland," somewhere around Coldfoot.

The hardy northern spruce

These trees may fall into the "Charlie Brown Christmas tree" end of the spectrum, but considering the conditions in which they survive, I think they are pretty magnificent.

I finally got back to the spot where I had dropped my sunglasses and pulled off to look for them. I parked and walked a long loop around the parking lot. They were nowhere to be found. I looked up to a most unexpected sight—a middle-aged man pushing a bicycle with a small trailer attached to the back of it. Ordinarily, a man on a bike isn't unusual, but remember, the only road ahead was the Dalton Highway. There was nothing for the next several hundred miles but gravel, dirt, and approaching semis.

I waved to him, and he smiled and rolled his bike over toward me.

"Howdy," he said, and I couldn't quite place the accent.

"Hey." I turned and gave a look at the long, straight

stretch of road ahead, then back at his bike.

"You heading up the Dalton? There's not much up that way." I glanced at the sun. It was already past 8 p.m., and even though it got dark later this far north, it would only be a couple of hours to twilight.

"Yep," he said. "That's the way I like it. My buddy's got a cabin up ahead a few miles, and he lets me stay at it."

I replayed the last fifty miles of road in my mind and couldn't recall any spur roads that led off the main highway, or any sign of a cabin.

"Like your solitude, eh?"

He nodded and grinned, showing a lot of missing teeth. He didn't have a care in the world.

"Would you like a ride? It'll be dark in a few hours."

He looked at me like I was crazy.

"Ride? Nah. I like my bike. I just went down to get some supplies," he said, jerking a thumb at his trailer.

"Good enough, then. Good luck."

He smiled and waved again and started pushing his bike north on the highway.

I love Alaskans.

I never did find those sunglasses.

When I checked into my motel in Fairbanks, I did what I always do—opened my laptop and prepared to update my blog. There was an interesting message in my inbox, though, from a producer who works for the A&E network. The message said he was working on a project about America, and he wanted to know if I might be interested in consulting on the show.

My first thought was, "Which of my friends is trying to pull a fast one on me?" But a quick Google search revealed that he was legit.

After several emails and a long phone conversation, it was settled. Just like that, I was a travel consultant for the A&E network, which presents many of my favorite shows. It was an exciting, fun challenge, but it would be slightly difficult to pull off while traveling through Alaska, since they needed my input, essentially, yesterday.

I realized that sometime over the next week, I'd have to take a day off the road to work on this project, but who can say "no" to television? Certainly not me.

Day Nine

"It's not like Alaska isn't wilderness—it mostly is. But most Alaskans don't live in the wild. They live on the edge of the wild in towns with schools and cable TV and stores and dentists and roller rinks sometimes. It's just like anyplace else, only with mountains and moose." —Tom Bodett

If every day was as jam-packed as this one, I'd drop from exhaustion. Still, a great day.

I woke up in Fairbanks, which seems like a nice town. A city by Alaska standards, of course, but just a town anywhere else in the U.S.A. One thing that struck me about Fairbanks is how spread out it is. It feels like it's the size of Seattle, geography-wise, but it has only about five percent of Seattle's population. I think that's probably a function of land being relatively inexpensive here, whereas it is very dear in the Seattle Metro area.

Before I left Fairbanks, I wanted to check out Blue Babe. Nope, not Babe the Blue Ox of Paul Bunyan fame, but Blue Babe, the amazingly well-preserved remains of an Alaska steppe bison, an extinct species that once roamed Europe, northern Asia and North America. Here's what Blue Babe looks like, as preserved in the Alaska Museum of the North, at the University of Alaska:

The *other* Babe

The remains of Blue Babe were found during a mining operation in 1979. The miners, Walter and Ruth Roman, recognized that they had found something unusual, and called the university to preserve it. When carbon dating was done, Blue Babe was found to be 36,000 years old. The mummified body was so well-preserved that, based on teeth and puncture marks, scientists were even able to determine how it died—killed by an Ice Age American lion, which must have been pretty huge to bring down something like this all alone.

Babe the Steppe Bison probably died just as the weather turned very cold, and so the body froze and was maintained in immaculate condition for 360 centuries. I spent a long time staring at it, trying to imagine the world it lived and died in.

The rest of the Museum of the North is excellent too,

and it's just the right size for a visit, with excellent displays on local wildlife, history, and culture. Admission is only $12, and if you're in Fairbanks, I highly recommend it.

After I spent an hour or two in the museum, I headed south, as I had many sites to see before slept.

My next stop was Healy, Alaska. As is true of most rural Alaska towns, there's not much to Healy. It's more of a wide spot in the road with a few businesses: a gas station, small store, a restaurant or two. One of those restaurants is the 49th State Brewing Company, which, like many businesses that cater mostly to travelers, hadn't opened for the season yet. When I pulled into the parking lot, there was a lot of activity, with workmen, power tools, and other people bustling about, so I assumed they were planning to reopen soon. Nonetheless, I was able to see what I came to see.

First was this very cool signpost, with arrows pointing toward many locations, indicating the appropriate mileage:

It doesn't say how far to Seaside, Washington, though

At the top, you'll note a sign that says, "Magic Bus, 35 miles" It's a reference to the bus Chris McCandless, whose story was told in *Into the Wild,* found in the Alaska wilderness. The book and movie *Into the Wild* tell the story of a well-off young man who rejected society and its rules and walked off to live in the wilderness. He came across an abandoned Fairbanks city bus that a construction company had left behind and set up camp there.

Eventually, he starved to death, which many locals felt was inevitable because of the scant provisions he'd taken with him and his lack of survival knowledge. The movie suggests he poisoned himself by eating deadly berries, but that seems not to have been the case. The bus has come to be known as "the magic bus" and it draws many visitors, who make the hike out to it as a kind of pilgrimage.

That hike is long, more than ten miles, and potentially

dangerous—one person died while crossing a river on the way a few years ago—so I had no interest in attempting it. Still, I am interested in the story, so I stopped to see the full-size replica that director Sean Penn had built for the movie, which is on display at 49th State Brewing Company.

Not all movie props are beautiful

The real "magic bus" that sits in the wilderness doesn't look much like it did when Chris McCandless found it. Those hikers and pilgrims like to take a little piece of their shrine back home with them, so the bus has been stripped down to the bare nubbins and has been covered in graffiti. This bus, sitting in a restaurant parking lot, actually looks more like the original once did, both inside and out.

A Lap Around Alaska

Roughing it, Hollywood-style.

Yes, it was just a replica, but it was cool to see it, and driving around the town of Healy gave me a better perspective on what Chris McCandless saw as the last outpost of civilization.

About 100 miles south of Healy is Denali National Park, the one and only national park I was expecting to hit directly on this road trip. Last summer, Dawn and I visited more than a dozen national parks on our trip around the Lower 48, but Alaska is different. It has no shortage of national parks, but accessing them can be a little tricky and often requires an airplane, helicopter, or boat. This trip, I was concentrating only on areas that I could access via car, so my national park exposure was bound to be limited.

Denali is an immense park. At 1.33 million acres, it is bigger even than Yellowstone, but accessibility isn't nearly as good. In Yellowstone, there are paved roads that will loop you through the entire park. Today, I was able to drive only about 30 miles into the park, once again because it was so early in the season. As the weather warms, more roads open and access is better, but even in mid-summer, the vast majority of the park is reachable only by flightseeing on a small plane. It truly is a wilderness.

The big attraction in Denali is the mountain of the same name, the tallest in North America at more than 20,000 feet. Mount Denali is about 80 miles south of the park road, though, and even on a relatively clear day, the peak is likely to hide behind clouds. That was the case for me. I kept my eye peeled in Denali's direction for the whole drive into the park, and I pulled over at every lookout that promised a view, but it was for naught. Denali hid behind her clouds like a nervous bride behind her veil.

Really, Denali is there. Behind the clouds

That mountain in the foreground is called Double Mountain. To the right, where all the clouds are, is where Denali is. I drove the road for hours, and never got a better shot of the mountain than this.

By the way, if you are of a certain age, you might know Denali by a different name: Mount McKinley. It was named after the twenty-fifth president by a gold prospector in 1898, but of course, indigenous peoples had been living there for many centuries before that. They had long ago named the mountain "Denali," after the Koyukon word *Deenaalee,* which means "high one." When I visited Alaska in the mid-'70s, there was already an argument raging about the name. The federal government lined up behind McKinley, while many Alaskans just went on calling it Denali. Finally, in 2015, it became official at the federal level.

Denali National Park was just waking up for the season, and it seemed that way as I drove through it. It felt like being the first person in a large department store on a Monday morning. There was virtually no traffic, and I saw no wildlife, but I might have been surrounded and missed it because I needed to keep my eyes on the road. Even without Mount Denali or wildlife appearances, the park is a jewel, with amazing scenery that changes every mile. I would like to come back and tour it again in warmer weather.

I could have said this every day, but on this day I found another section of road where the scenery was so beautiful, it was slightly overwhelming. I drove south on the Parks Highway through the small village of Cantwell, and a few miles past that, I was surrounded on all four sides by towering, snow-capped peaks.

The Talkeetna Mountains, alongside the Parks Highway

I've mentioned before that I don't do a lot of planning for my road trips, and that's true. However, in the weeks and months leading up to the trip, I do often surf the web, looking for unusual oddities that I can investigate. South of the village of Cantwell, I found one of my favorites for this trip: Igloo City. It's not a real igloo, and it's not a city, but it is hopelessly cool.

All because one man dared to dream

I am attracted to people who tilt at windmills, dreamers who have an outsized vision and do everything in their power to make it happen. The *other* JFK, whom I met last year and who has the world's largest ball of twine, springs to mind. Or Robert Asp, the Minnesotan who built a Viking ship to sail to Norway. I love those guys.

To that list, you can add Leon Smith, who dreamed of building an 80-foot-tall igloo in the middle of the Alaska wilderness and opening it as a hotel. He got partway there. As you can see, he got the multistory igloo built for the most part, but he never finished it. Did he run out of money? Lose interest? Realize he was building a giant igloo in the middle of nowhere? I have no idea. The most credible story I can find said that he fell ill and was unable to complete it.

Like everything else in this part of Alaska, the surroundings were covered in a foot or more of frosty snow, but I pulled on my boots and hiked up to the building for a better look. It's never been finished, and it sits on the side of the road like the ghost of an unfulfilled dream, now nothing more than a target for vandals and graffiti artists:

Kilroy was here

If you look closely at that picture, you can see that there is a concrete block to discourage people from sneaking inside, but to the right of that, someone has ripped away enough of the boards that a very skinny person could sneak inside. I am not a very skinny person. I did, however, stick my camera inside and take a picture:

A Lap Around Alaska

A little paint and it will be good as new

I thought of sticking my head in for a better look around, but some very strange, scratching sounds emanated from deep in the bowels of the igloo. I'm sure it was rats or some other small wildlife that have found a relatively warm and dry spot out of the snow. You know what, though? I didn't stick around to investigate. I hotfooted it back to the Emerald Bullet and headed down the road.

Back on the Parks Highway, I found a spot touted as a great location to see Mount Denali. I was game, so I pulled over and walked out to the viewing area. It wasn't great, but it was the best shot of Denali I was going to get on this day:

If you squint, you can see the former Mount McKinley

As I stood to take that picture, I watched an interesting scene play out in front of me. To my left were three tourists speaking French as they looked toward the mountain. I took two years of French in high school and I can't remember how to say anything other than "Je m'appelle Shawn," but at least I can recognize the language when it is spoken. To my right was a man standing on top of the barrier that encircled the viewing area.

I looked at him, looked at the mountain, fifty miles away, then looked back at it him. It was hard for me to extrapolate how the extra two feet of height he was getting made it worth risking a tumble onto the hillside below. Most people would have kept their mouth shut. I am not most people.

"Sorry, I've got to ask, but does that extra couple of feet really change the perspective on your shot?"

He didn't take the camera away from his eye, but said, "I'm trying to take a video of the mountain, but," and here he raised his voice into a peevish tone, "some people just won't shut up."

At first, I assumed he was talking about me, because when people say, "won't shut up," they're usually looking at me. At that moment, the man took his eye away from his camera and jerked his head toward the three tourists, including me in a brotherhood I had no interest in joining. Under his breath, he added, "And they can't even speak English."

"Oh, I see," I said. I contemplated asking him the reason why he wanted to take a video of a static object, but I managed to suppress that. At that point, again, most people would have just left.

I walked over to the tourists and struck up a conversation. "Well, what do you think of the mountain?" and, "Would you like to pose in front of it and have me take your picture?" They spoke English quite well, far better than I would speak French in Paris, and we had a nice conversation that went on for several long minutes. Eventually, the angry man gave up and stomped back to his car.

I often think that if I don't tick at least one person off in a day, then I'm just not trying very hard. Glad to see that I met my quota, at least for today.

It had been a full day, starting with Blue Babe and ending with the angry videographer. I made my way down to Wasilla and found a hotel room. As soon as I mention I stayed in the small town of Wasilla, I inevitably get two questions, so I'll answer them now. No, I didn't see Sarah Palin pumping gas or at the grocery store, and, no, I couldn't see Russia from my porch.

Day Ten

As I've aged, I have noticed that some things just don't come as easily. I'm not ancient, but at fifty-seven, I can tell things are changing. One of those is the physical and mental stamina I had three or four decades ago.

In the summer of 1981, I was traveling on the Unlimited Hydroplane circuit. I was staying at the Executive Inn in Evansville, Indiana, where we had just wrapped up a Thunder on the Ohio event. My sister Terri called me late one night and told me she had two tickets to see Pat Benatar at the Coliseum in Seattle. The only issue was, the concert was less than two days away, and we were halfway across the country. My best friend, Ian, my partner in crime on the circuit, immediately jumped up and started throwing his clothes into his knapsack.

"What are we waiting for?" he asked.

"Bro," I said, because that's what we called each other back in the '80s, "We're in Indiana. There's no way we get to Seattle before the concert." The issue was complicated by the fact that Ian didn't drive. That meant I would have to drive, non-stop, more than 2,200 miles, then muster the energy to enjoy a Billy Squier/Pat Benatar double bill.

Long story short, we made it with a few hours to spare. We never stopped for anything other than fuel and bathroom breaks. The kicker was, when the concert was over (Pat was incredible; I wasn't all that crazy about Billy Squier) I didn't even feel tired. That's what it was like being twenty-one years old.

Why do I mention this? Mostly because I'd been pushing myself pretty hard since I left Seaview ten days ago. Not only had I averaged more than 400 miles per day, but *a lot* of those miles were over roads that any sane person wouldn't drive. On this day,

I discovered once and for all that I am no longer twenty-one years old.

When I woke up at 5:15 a.m., I could barely move. Maybe I should say, I didn't really *want* to move. Instead of being up and on the road by 6:30 as I normally am, I was still lying in bed at 8 a.m. Eventually, I did get up and motor on down the road a few miles, but I knew when I got to Anchorage, which is just a short drive from Wasilla, that I was done for the day. Gotta learn to pace myself a little bit, I guess.

I did find a couple of cool things on the road, along with the spectacular scenery I have now come to expect from Alaska. Somewhere along the Glenn Highway, I pulled off into the small native village of Eklutna. Eklutna isn't big, but it is hardy—it's been continually occupied for 367 years.

In the 1830s, Russian missionaries built this little church:

Russian Orthodox church in Eklutna

If you're thinking it looks pretty good for a church that's 180 years old, that's because it was remodeled about fifty years ago. The old Russian Orthodox church is obviously very cool, but it's the cemetery that is attached to it that puts it over the top:

Burial spirit houses

Those brightly colored little houses are actually burial spirit houses. The traditions of the Russian Orthodox church combined with the traditions of the indigenous Dana'ina people who populate the town, and this is the result. At first, I thought it was a little odd that many of the burial houses are in such poor repair. I wondered why that was. Had the families moved away or died out? A little research revealed that the native culture believes that things that come from the earth should eventually be allowed to return to the earth, so they do no maintenance, and instead let the small houses crumble back into the earth over time.

Another thing I noticed was the unusual crosses that decorated most of the spirit houses:

A Russian Orthodox cross

Apparently, the top crossbar represents the inscription over Christ's head, the middle bar His outstretched arms, and the lower bar His footrest. I don't know if this is common to Russian Orthodox, or somewhat unusual, but I'd never seen it before.

I left Eklutna and headed south to Anchorage. My memory of the Matanuska Valley is that it was one of the most pristine, gorgeous places on the planet, and these past two days had confirmed that. I felt privileged to have had the opportunity to explore it once again. If you choose to read my story, *My Matanuska Summer,* which will follow at the end of this book, this is the area I camped out during that spectacular, wasted summer.

By late afternoon, I was already checked into my motel room in Anchorage. This was the first city I ever saw in Alaska, back in 1974, when I first flew in to visit my brother. I'm sure the city has grown a lot over the intervening forty-three years, but it had the same vibe to me now that it did then. As I previously wrote about Fairbanks, Anchorage is a city—the largest in Alaska—but it still feels a bit like a town. It's easy to get around in, and the traffic isn't bad at all.

What it does have is lots of big stores, so I took the opportunity to restock the Magical Mystery Bag and collapse into another one in my endless series of cheap motels.

Day Eleven

This was my day to devote to the A&E project, titled *America Close Up*. By the time you are reading this book, the project may very well be out, because the production was on a fast track. Or, typical of how these things work, it may still be in development. Either way, after this day, my part in it was relatively complete.

America Close Up is a show meant to highlight America and where it finds itself in the twenty-first century. I was hired because they searched on Amazon for "American road trips," and *A Lap Around America* was at the top of the list. Thank you, Amazon, for the recommendation. My job was to help match some of the ideas they wanted to illustrate with actual locations in the United States where they might consider shooting. Having spent two months traveling those very places last year, it was a consulting job right up my alley.

By the end of the day, I hadn't moved a single mile in the Emerald Bullet, but I had completed my recommendations for the show. I am proud of the work I did, and hope it will help them create something excellent.

The next day, it would be back to the lap around Alaska. Seward and the rest of the Kenai Peninsula were in my sights now. Since that's where I spent most of my time back in the '70s, I'd been looking forward to seeing how my memories matched up with present-day realities.

Day Twelve

Following my report on this epic road trip, I am including two short memoirs that cover the two summers I spent in Alaska forty years ago. In the first of those two stories, called *Diver I,* I wrote about my first impressions of the drive between Anchorage and Seward, circa 1975:

I goggled at the scenery the whole drive to Seward. I had always thought that Mossyrock was rural, but it was civilized compared with Chugach National Forest. Mile after mile after mile of hills, towering mountains, trees and, even though it was June, a lot of snow-capped peaks.

That paragraph was based on a four-decades-old memory, but it absolutely fits. Here's a bit of what I saw on this day's drive:

Cook Inlet

One other strong memory I have from more than forty years ago: The first time I flew into Anchorage, when we broke through the top layer of clouds, I looked down to see mountaintops peeking through another layer of fog and clouds. At the time, being a young and inexperienced traveler and not knowing anything about Alaska, I wondered if the snow really piled up so high that it covered everything except for the peaks of the mountains. I thought of that today, when I saw these peaks getting lost in the clouds above me.

Definitely clouds, not snow

Spring was here in south-central Alaska, but the melt-off was a work in progress. I saw a lot of lakes and rivers that were starting to lose the ice and snow, but there was a long way to go. Every few miles, I saw, and heard, small runoff waterfalls tumbling down hillsides, which makes for a lovely and melodic drive.

An odd thing happened as I drew closer to Seward—things started to look familiar. Yes, I had spent a lot of time in Seward, but that was so many years ago, I expected that everything would be foreign to me. That wasn't the case. I recognized certain curves in the road and hills that butted right up against the shoulder with the sense that I'd seen them only yesterday.

Everything looked so familiar, I was feeling nostalgic. Then I got to Seward Harbor, and—holy crap. The last time I saw Seward Harbor, it was a beautiful little spot with a nice mixture of commercial fishing boats and pleasure boats. It was quiet. If you wanted to go to the store or to get something to eat, you had to drive into Seward proper. Not any more.

The harbor is now like a second small town adjacent to Seward. There are restaurants, souvenir shops, coffee shops, ice cream shops, charter fishing outfits and anything else that might appeal to tourists. The harbor and breakwater have been greatly expanded from the last time I was there. I learned that cruise ships—the big ones—now stop at Seward. That would have been inconceivable back in the '70s.

In a slight daze, I parked the car and wandered out among the boats, trying to get my bearings. That's when I saw these guys:

We like to have our picture taken

Few things on the planet are as much fun to watch as sea otters at play. When I was on a crabber in 1974, we often had otters that would swim alongside us, playing tag and other ridiculous games. I immediately felt like I was home again.

I kept trying to get my bearings and recall where everything had been in 1974. Finally, I found a building I recognized, got my bearings, and realized just how much the harbor had expanded.

Like other tourist-oriented businesses in Alaska, Seward Harbor was just coming awake for the season. A lot of the shops and restaurants were still closed, but I saw activity inside them as they prepped for another busy summer ahead.

I wandered into a tourist shop and booked a four-hour whale cruise for the next day. It would be a different type of boat, of course, but I thought sailing out of the Seward Harbor breakwater would feel much the way it had decades earlier.

Another of my other strong memories of Seward was a store called the Alaska Shop. Before I left, I had Googled it, certain that it would be gone, but I was thrilled to see it was still open for business. It was my first stop in Seward proper. Here's how I describe it in the mini-memoir, *Diver I:*

I knew I'd found my Nirvana as soon as we walked in. The left side of the store was an old-fashioned soda fountain, with green countertops and red spinning stools. To the right of that was a wide selection of magazines, comics, and books. As if that wasn't enough, beside that was a huge selection of candy bars. I glanced beyond the candy and saw that there were a bunch of touristy displays and knickknacks, but I couldn't have cared less about a clock made out of a burl with a moose attached to it. Burgers, comics, and candy were my holy trinity, and they were all here, under one roof.

I had carried that memory of the Alaska Shop with me ever since. And so I was crushed when I walked in and found … just an ordinary store. No soda fountain, no long racks of magazines and candy that would catch the eye of any young boy. Just jewelry and souvenirs.

I remembered the store as being open and spacious, with high ceilings and an atmosphere that invited you to come in and spend your hard-earned money. Now it felt dark and a bit dingy. I asked the young girl behind the counter if there was anyone who had been around the store for a long time. She nodded at a man who appeared to be a few years older than me in the corner, putting away inventory.

"Hi," I said, approaching him. "Have you been here a long time?"

"Yep," he nodded. "Since the early '80s. I own the place."

"Am I imagining things, or did there used to be a soda fountain along this wall?" I asked, pointing toward the back.

"Oh." He paused, remembering. "Yes, of course. I took that out. Couldn't ever find good help to keep it going."

I looked at the low ceilings, the dark lighting, and the inventory that no fourteen-year-old boy would ever be interested in. "Thanks," I said. "Appreciate the information."

Most of the time, you really can't go home again. I walked out of the store and knew I would never need to go back. The Alaska Shop of my childhood still exists, if only in my memory.

I walked around the block. It was getting late, and I needed to find a place to lay my head. Just around the corner was a Best Western, sleek and modern-looking. Except I still have my rule: no corporations, if at all possible.

I glanced up the street. The Hotel Seward beckoned, a place old enough that it had already appeared slightly decrepit forty years earlier. I noted happily that it looked like some renovations had been done over the years. Best of all, it definitely wasn't a corporate hotel.

I walked into the lobby, which is a story in itself—with enough historic artifacts and stuffed animals to fill a small museum. I asked the young woman behind the counter if they had a room for the night.

    "Historic wing, or the Alaska wing?"

    "I don't know. What's the difference?"

    "Well, the Alaska wing has a private bathroom."

    "And the Historic wing?"

    "… doesn't."

    "Doesn't?"

    "Doesn't have a private bath. You'll be sharing a bathroom with several other rooms."

In my younger days, I'm sure I would have been more up for the adventure of sharing a bathroom with complete strangers, but these days I prefer at least minimal creature comforts, such as not having to bump into room 217 on the way to the bathroom in the middle of the night.

    "I'll take the Alaska wing, thank you."

    "It's $12 more per night."

    "And worth every penny."

The Alaska wing was added on to the historic Hotel Seward within the last twenty years, and it was actually very nice. I crossed the street to a small restaurant that had provided my first meal in Seward forty years ago. Still open, still good food.

Day Thirteen

I was back on the early-riser schedule, now that I'd had a few days to rest up from my road fatigue. I was up, showered, and walking around Seward by 7 a.m. It was brisk, you might even say cool, but the beautiful experience of watching the sun rise over the mountains that ring Resurrection Bay, then shine on the Seward Mountains behind me, made braving the chill absolutely worth it.

Sunrise on the Seward Mountains

My first goal of the day was to walk Seward from one end to the other, trying to see how much I could recognize. My first discovery was a sad one. In the '70s, life was never boring in Seward, but there weren't a lot of entertainment options, especially when you were fourteen or fifteen. There was a slab of concrete behind the Hotel Seward where I used to play pickup basketball games, and there was the Liberty Theater.

It was at the Liberty that I first saw *Young Frankenstein*. I loved it so much that I walked out of the theater, bought another ticket and watched it a second time. I also remember seeing *Deliverance* there with my brother, Mick, and being pretty creeped out by the whole thing. Banjo music still makes me nervous all these years later. I was thinking I might even try to catch a show there, just for old times' sake.

The Liberty Theater, a little too late

I was disappointed when I saw that the movie being advertised was *Last Vegas,* a movie from a few years back. The Liberty had obviously been closed since then. It was really tough on small theaters when the studios required them to switch over to digital, as that was an expensive process. I knew it would put many small theaters out of business, and it did, including the Liberty.

My Matanuska Summer, also included at the end of this book, tells the story of what happened to me in the summer of 1976, including the none-too-exciting job of painting apartments. For what it's worth, I thought I would include a shot of the building where I toiled, slapping ugly green paint on walls for $5 per hour:

Yep, still ugly

I never said it was beautiful, right? Here's something I have always found beautiful, though:

Seward's own Mount Marathon

Mount Marathon isn't much when it comes to height—it's only a touch over 3,000 feet. What makes it special is the Mount Marathon race, held every Fourth of July. Crazy, incredibly in-shape people race to the top of that mountain and back down in around 43 minutes. The whole race started, as so many great things do, as a bar bet more than a century ago, when one man bet another that he could make it to the top and back in under an hour. He wasn't able to do it in the allotted time, but many, many runners do it routinely these days.

I watched several Mount Marathon races in the '70s, and even then, it wasn't unusual for runners to finish the race battered and bleeding. The reason is simple—they spend almost all their time pushing *up* the mountain. Once there, they descend in leaps and bounds, which is fast but dangerous. If I were anywhere in Alaska over the Fourth of

July, I would make it a point to be in Seward for this race.

After my trip down memory lane in Seward, I headed back to Seward Harbor for my whale- watching adventure. I've mentioned how stunning the harbor is, but I wanted to share a picture for reference.

Mountains and masts in Seward Harbor

The weather forecast called for rain, but instead we were blessed with sunshine and blue skies. I was scheduled to board the *Glacier Explorer* at noon. By 11:45, I was making new friends while standing in line to board. One, named Bravo, was a young woman from Texas who traveled all over the country for her work. Talking to her in line, I could see she took full advantage of the travel opportunities. She didn't just sit in her hotel room in whatever city she was in, she got out and saw what there was to see, a trait I can admire.

Behind us in line was a couple, slightly older than me,

from Homer, which is on the other side of the Kenai Peninsula. They said they drove to Seward every year to take an excursion like this. The four of us ended up sitting together and chatting for much of the four-hour cruise. Fast friendships are often made when strangers are thrown together in an enclosed space.

The captain of the *Glacier Explorer* made a long announcement that, I think, covered the safety rules and other aspects of travel through Resurrection Bay. I say "I think" because the sound coming from a speaker above our heads was so distorted that the entire speech sounded like Charlie Brown's teacher. No matter, I got the gist of it: don't drown. Got it.

Moments later, the engines throbbed to life and we headed for the gap in the breakwater that would admit us to the bay. We were barely through the opening when I saw the first photo opportunity of the day.

Bald eagle with a fresh kill

It was a moment of strong déjà vu. I have a clear memory of seeing a bald eagle sitting in that same spot the first time I passed the breakwater on the *Diver I*. For a brief moment, I felt fourteen years old again, headed out to sea for the first time. Then I stood up, felt the crick in my back, and remembered I am definitely not fourteen any more.

A few hundred yards beyond the eagle we found an otter swimming alongside us on his back, playing hide-and-seek.

This turned out to be one of the best wildlife-spotting opportunities I had on the whole trip. I'd been keeping my eyes peeled for mountain goats along the way, but had yet to see so much as a disappearing hoof. Less than half an hour into the trip, I finally spotted one on the cliffs as we chugged by. He was a good distance away and I had the little telephoto lens on my camera maxed out, but I did manage to get a shot of him.

Master of all he surveys

Directly below the mountain goat was a rock so covered with sleeping sea lions, it looked like a frat house the morning after a kegger:

A hard day's night

Two hours into the cruise, we had seen a wide variety of wildlife but no whales. Someone said they had seen one blow off to the port side; the captain stopped the ship and we waited for several long minutes, but it never resurfaced.

Finally, we found whale heaven—a whole pod, swimming together. If I were a better nature photographer, I'm sure I would have gotten many great shots of them. Instead, I spent much of the time just leaning on the railing, watching them cavort and play. I did manage to grab one shot that shows four whales all together.

Hard to capture, as they move quickly

This is as good as any time to talk about living life through a lens. I was conscious the entire trip of my desire to capture great pictures, both for this book and for my own memories. At the same time, I didn't want to be the kind of person who misses the forest because there's a shot of a tree in front of him. As important as photographs are, in other words, there are times to put the camera away and see the broader perspective.

My cruise on the *Glacier Explorer* was one of those times. I'm glad I got the chance to capture the bald eagle, the mountain goat, and the sea lions and whales on my camera card, but even more, I'm glad I got to stand on the deck of the boat and feel the waves beneath my feet, smell the bracing salt air, and see the incredible open vistas of Resurrection Bay and the Gulf of Alaska.

When we docked back in Seward, I said goodbye to

Bravo and the older couple with whom I had spent several hours reminiscing about Alaska in the good old days. It was nice being back on solid land again, but almost immediately, I missed the sea.

I spent one more night in the Hotel Seward, which had been a nice headquarters for my visit to my old stomping grounds. It's changed a lot over the past four decades, which is inevitable, but it's still essentially the same small town I fell in love with. My best advice is, if you are planning a tour of Alaska, be sure to include a visit to the Kenai Peninsula, and Seward in particular. It's a wonderful little town.

Day Fourteen

I woke up in Seward feeling a little sad to leave. This visit had felt a bit like going home. The town may have changed, but the mountains, bay, and scenery are the same, and they stir my soul. I dawdled for a bit around town, not wanting to leave. The rain promised the previous day finally arrived in force, though, and that put me on the road.

I had one more tourist stop to make before I left, at the local memorial to the 1964 earthquake that shook, rattled, and rolled Alaska. It's not much to look at—just a boat anchor and a plaque. I'm not 100 percent sure how the anchor came to symbolize the earthquake, but there we are.

There aren't many precise moments from more than fifty years ago at which I remember exactly where I was, but 6:36 p.m. Pacific Time, on March 27, 1964, is one. I was only four years old, but I have a clear memory of sitting on the floor in the bedroom I shared with my big brother, Mickey, who was fourteen at the time. I remember bumping up and down as though I was sitting on a trampoline someone else was jumping on. We had some small built-in shelves against one wall, and all the little knickknacks on them came tumbling down. It seemed to go on for a long time, but eventually, Mom came in and scooped me up.

That was in Riffe, Washington, a town that no longer exists, as it was flooded when the Mossyrock Dam opened. I was approximately 2,400 miles away from the epicenter of that Good Friday earthquake. That's what happens when a 9.1 temblor (the second strongest ever recorded) occurs.

Much of Alaska was devastated, first by the earthquake, then the tsunamis that swept over shores and harbors. It was so powerful that parts of Kodiak, to the southwest, were raised thirty feet almost instantly. Some 139 people died, mostly because of the tsunamis.

You can still see the aftereffects of the earthquake, even fifty-three years later. On the whale cruise, we passed a sandbar on which stood several dead trees. The captain said they died when the quake moved the land six feet, flooding the trees with saltwater and killing them, while simultaneously preserving them.

On the way out of town, I visited Seward Harbor one last time, drawn like steel to a magnet. Even though I'd spent a lot of time walking around the harbor, I hadn't been to the spot where I'd spent much of the summer of '74, aboard the docked World War II vessel called the *Diver I,* which had been converted into a crabber.

Using the few old landmarks that remained in the harbor, I found exactly where the *Diver I* had been tied up.

One last shot of Seward Harbor

The *Diver I* was a much bigger boat than those seen in the picture—it was 107 feet stem to stern, and much taller. I remember being able to step right off the dock and across onto the boat, which freaked me out a little bit the first few times I did it, as there was always a small gap between the two.

Having satisfied that particular itch, I took off for Soldotna.

When I first planned this trip, I contemplated making it a true lap around Alaska—hitting the Panhandle, which is only easily accessible by boat or plane, then taking several other excursions out into the Alaskan bush, into towns and areas that are reachable only by float plane. In the end, though, I scaled the trip back by dividing it into three parts: roads, boats, and planes.

I plan to return and make a lap of the entire Alaska Marine Highway System, which actually starts in Bellingham, Washington, and goes up the Panhandle and across the Aleutian Islands. That will definitely be a trip all its own.

Then I plan on a third trip, basing myself in Anchorage and Fairbanks and taking excursions to the most remote parts of Alaska via plane.

That left this trip as the true "road" trip. On this morning, looking at my maps, I realized that it wouldn't be too long before I ran out of roads to cover. Alaska is an immense state, but much of it has no highway system at all. If you really, truly, want to go off the grid, there is plenty of opportunity to do just that in Alaska.

This day, I planned on driving to Soldotna, then south to Homer the next. That's absolutely as far as you can go in that direction, because you run out of road at the end of the Homer Spit. After that, I decided, I'd hop over to Valdez, just because I'd never been there before. And with that I would have covered most of the interconnected roads available to motorists in Alaska.

Already, the end of this trip was in sight. After Valdez, I

planned to drive back through Tok, then head east into Canada toward Watson Lake. Instead of taking the AlCan all the way back to Dawson Creek, I decided to drive south on Highway 37 because of its reputation for excellent wildlife viewing.

The trip from Seward to Soldotna was picturesque, with mountains, lakes, and rivers. If there are ugly parts of Alaska, I didn't see them on this trip.

Most lakes are still frozen at the end of April

Once I got to Soldotna, I ended up needing to do some more work on the A&E project, so I didn't get much of a chance to look around. However, I can say that the Soldotna of 2017 bears very little resemblance to the town I remember in the 1970s. Back then, it was a tiny town of approximately 1,000 people. Today, it is four times that, and it feels much larger, as there are Walmart and Fred Meyer stores there now.

Day Fifteen

I'm sure that Soldotna is a great place to live, but as I drove around the area looking for points of interest, I didn't find much. So I drove on north to Kenai. For the past week, everywhere I'd gone, I seemed to be surrounded by mountains on all sides. So about halfway to Kenai, it felt odd to experience a little elbow room and some open space.

Kenai feels as flat as Kansas after all the mountains I've seen

My longtime friend and cover artist, Linda Boulanger, grew up in the Kenai area, so I tried to scamper around and find places she remembered from her childhood. As I sent her photos from my phone, she lamented that the present-day reality didn't look as wonderful as the photographs in her mind. That's the truth for most of us. Our memories embroider places with emotion, while stark reality can be so plain.

I visited another old Russian Orthodox church in Kenai. I love their spires and classic designs. This one was built in 1894 and is a registered national historic landmark. It is called the Holy Assumption of the Virgin Mary Russian Orthodox Church, which is quite a mouthful when people ask you where you go to church.

"I go to the church with the blue spires" is probably easier

After an hour or two tooling around Kenai, I backtracked toward Soldotna and headed south.

Ever since I got on the AlCan almost two weeks earlier, I'd kept my eyes peeled for moose. I'd passed dozens and dozens of "moose crossing" signs. But, until this day, I hadn't seen so much as a single Bullwinkle. Then, a few miles north of Anchor Point, I turned around a bend, and there they were.

You lookin' at me?

I know it looks like I was standing right next to this moose, but that's thanks to the telephoto lens. I made sure I was always a safe distance away from all the wildlife, especially those big enough to walk over me without even noticing.

My wildlife bingo card now had only one empty square: bear. I hoped to get a chance to fill that gaping hole before I get back to Washington. Ironically, while I was in bear country in Alaska, Dawn, back home, had an encounter with a small black bear while walking the dogs. In Seaview, they come out at night and rifle through garbage cans, looking for tasty bits. Also, while I'd been gone, our cat had taken to bringing corpses into the house. I think our kitty was worried that Dawn might not be able to provide for everyone while I was gone. In any case, between the black bears and the dead rodents, I was pretty sure she'd be glad when I finally got home.

Just past the moose, I made a quick stop in Anchor Point.

Westward, ho

In the past year, I really have made a Lap Around America. On this day, I was at the most westerly point you can reach by road. The previous week, in Coldfoot, I'd been within 200 miles of the most northerly point in the United States. The previous September, I'd been in Key West, Florida, the most southerly point. And, in October, we were in Maine, just a few hundred miles from the most easterly point. No wonder I'm tired.

Having seen the height and breadth of what the United States has to offer, I remain optimistic about our great nation. There is a feeling that we are politically divided, and a single scroll through your Facebook newsfeed will confirm that. If you take the time to travel the country, though, and stop and talk with people, it soon becomes clear—away from social media, we're all just people, with families and dreams for the future. I feel blessed to have seen this with my own eyes.

South of Anchor Point is Homer, the halibut capital of Alaska, and one of my favorite little towns.

The Homer Spit

Isn't that a lovely shot? That's Highway 1, heading into Homer, with the Homer Spit beyond, and mountains beyond that. Homer really is a jewel.

I wanted to drive the road as far as I could, so I drove out onto that spit, all the way to where the road stops.

A Lap Around Alaska

The end of the road

It's a cool experience to take a highway to its very end. That's the view from the spit, with a couple of fishing boats out on the water, enjoying the day.

I drove through Homer, which combines vintage and modern buildings, old shops and motels rubbing elbows with a McDonald's down on the highway. I checked into a funky little motel and went to the grocery store to replenish the Magical Mystery Bag. On the short drive to the motel, I saw another moose, right in the middle of town, grazing in the empty lot next to where I was staying. Only in Alaska. It felt like an outtake from *Northern Exposure*.

This was a turning point in the trip. I'd followed the road that started in Tok as far north as I could, then worked my way through southeast Alaska and all around the Kenai Peninsula. Tomorrow, I would head toward Valdez.

Day Sixteen

Much of the morning was spent backtracking over roads I drove just a few days ago. Usually, that's not my favorite thing, but since I don't know when I'll get back to this part of Alaska again, it was like a little victory lap around one of my favorite places in the world. Even though I had a long drive ahead of me to Valdez, I also wanted to try driving down some unmarked country roads, just to see what might be around the next bend.

I did just that, and about a quarter of a mile down a gravel road I saw a sign that read, "Four wheel drive only beyond this point." Hmmm. On the one hand, that probably means the road's about to get pretty rough, but on the other, what good is driving an all-wheel-drive Subaru if you're never going to get into the mud? If Dawn had been with me, I would have turned around right there and headed for the highway. She was happily oblivious in our little beach cabin in Seaview, though, so on I went.

It didn't take me long to discover why the sign was there. Deep ruts, long stretches of mud that made the gravel road a distant memory, and huge puddles so deep I wasn't certain I would come out on the other side. Eventually, I saw a sign for Bottenintnin Lake off to the right. I'd never heard of Bottenintnin Lake and had absolutely no idea how that would be pronounced, but I turned right anyway.

After another teeth-rattling quarter-mile, I came upon a beautiful little lake that was the perfect lunchtime spot. I pulled parallel to the lake, opened my door and gazed out at the ripples playing against the shore. The sun had broken through the patchy clouds and warmed my face as I watched two mallard ducks swimming in gentle circles thirty feet away.

Well worth risking a little mud to see

I was wrapping my head around one of life's little mysteries—*Why can salamanders regenerate a limb when they lose it, but humans can't?*—and eating a peanut butter and jelly sandwich and a banana. The tiny *bong* of an incoming Facebook message startled me from my reverie. I thought I was well outside of cellphone range or any other sign of dastardly technology.

I thumbed the screen on to look at the message. Sitting in this pristine wilderness, I really didn't care what someone was having for lunch, or what new political incontinence one of my friends was sharing, but some habits die hard. It was a posting from one of the real estate agents I had worked with for so many years: *We're learning about multiple*

offers and other contingencies at our office meeting today.
That meant that all the real estate agents I had worked with hand in hand for so many years were sitting in their comfortable office, giving their attention to a presentation on Multiple Listing Association forms and the best way to get an edge in this fast-moving market and ...

And, I turned my phone off and gave my attention back to the ducks, still slowly swimming in circles. A breeze ruffled my hair with just enough bite to remind that even though it was April, this was still Alaska. I had 200 more miles to put under my wheels before I stopped for the day, but I was in no hurry to get back on the road.

Eventually, I figured out that it would take eight hours of steady driving to make it to Valdez, so I gave up my place of solitude to rejoin the rest of the world. After ten days of driving around Alaska, I was becoming jaded to the spectacular scenery. After touring the Kenai Peninsula, I figured I'd seen the best of it and now could just coast down to Valdez and then make my way home.

Once again, I was wrong, wrong, wrong. After turning west on Highway 1 at Wasilla, I saw some of the most gorgeous vistas I witnessed on the entire trip. I ended up getting into Valdez late that night, because I constantly had to pull over and drink in the scenery.

Here's an example. This lake is starting to give up its ice field, but for the moment it is still mostly frozen, with a few threads of water spreading through it. The sun reflected off the melting ice, making it look like a shimmering jewel that changed colors, depending on the angle of vision.

It was even prettier in person

I spent the early part of the afternoon driving along a winding road beside the Matanuska River. Sometimes the river was almost level with me, and at other times, it snaked along a canyon floor of its own making.

The Matanuska River

Eventually, I came to the Matanuska Glacier, which, at twenty-seven miles long and four miles wide, is the largest glacier in the United States that you can reach via your car. If so inclined, you can get a pass to hike it. I was inclined to sit in my car and say, "Oh my gosh, that's huge!"

There's a glacier under all that snow

I read that in the summertime, when the cover of snow melts away, it is a deep blue, which would be spectacular to see—almost worth a return trip all by itself.

At Glenallen, I turned south on Highway 4 toward Valdez, and the road almost immediately began climbing. It had been warm enough to be shirtsleeves weather in the morning, but by the time I had crossed a few mountain passes, it got downright cold. I pulled over to take a picture of the frozen peaks, shrouded in fog, but it was a lazy wind, so I quickly thought better and retreated to the Emerald Bullet. A lazy wind, by the way, is a wind that is too lazy to go around you, so it goes right through you instead.

As I drove, I scanned the mountaintops, hoping to catch another glimpse of a mountain goat. Instead, I was surprised to see, in a small pond that was so cold it had large chunks of floating ice, a pair of swans swimming placidly through the floes.

Swans keeping the ice at bay

As I drew nearer to Valdez, I saw two beautiful waterfalls, one flowing freely, the other still trying to break free of the ice.

Bridal Veil Falls

The more free-flowing waterfall is called Bridal Veil Falls. When I posted about it in my blog that night, people from all over the country responded in posts and messages that they have a Bridal Veil Falls near them as well. I guess that speaks to the limited number of metaphors available a century or more ago for something long and flowing.

For some reason, the hotels and motels in Valdez were all booked up, so I ended up staying at the Best Western. The room was nice, but the front-desk service was lackadaisical at best. The young woman there was much more concerned with whatever she was doing on her phone than she was about getting me checked in. Eventually, she managed to tear herself away long enough to register me and hand me my key.

I shouldered my bags, which seemed to grow heavier the longer I was traveling, and made my way down the long hallway to my room. I inserted the key, pushed into the room—and immediately noticed there was already a suitcase on the bed, that the shower was running, and the bathroom door was cracked open.

I backed out of there in a hurry, shutting the door as quietly as possible, and trudged back to the front desk. I stood there for a long minute until the woman managed to once again tear her attention away from Candy Crush and said, "Yes?" There was a hint of annoyance in her voice that conveyed the idea, "I already checked you off my to-do list, buddy."

"I think you sent me to someone else's room. They were showering."

She looked at my key packet, shrugged, and swiped another key through her machine. "Sorry," she said, in a way that made me think she wasn't sorry at all, and that somehow this little mess-up was really my fault. This is why I like to stay at mom-and-pop motels, where the person who checks you in may well have something at stake in your happiness.

Or, maybe I'm just tired and a little grumpy. It could be either one.

Day Seventeen

I had thought this might be my last day in Alaska, but it didn't turn out that way. I could have easily made it into Canada, but once you cross the border, it's a pretty good stretch until you make the first town with a motel, so I gave up the ghost early and rested. It had been a rewarding stretch of stunning scenery, wildlife, and 45 mph roads, and I was ready to take a bit of a break before the final push for Washington State.

Before I left Valdez, though, I spent a few minutes rolling around the town. Valdez is the terminus of the Alaska Pipeline, but in my casual drives around town, I didn't see much sign of that. In most ways, it looked like all Alaska small towns—both beautiful and ugly.

Welcome to Valdez!

As transcendentally lovely as the scenery of the state is, the towns, from Fairbanks to Wasilla to Soldotna, are not pretty. Alaska, especially this time of year, during the ice breakup and runoff, is a muddy, dirty place, and it's hard to keep a city pristine under those conditions. Even though most towns and villages in Alaska sit in a jewel of a setting, as evidenced by the picture above, the streets and buildings are plain and utilitarian. Year-round, but especially at this time of year, a thick layer of grime and mud settles over every outdoor surface, which gives the towns a slightly neglected look, even though they're not. I truly do understand it. The weather conditions are harsh, and Alaskans seem to have more on their minds than constantly fighting an endless battle against the muck—like actually enjoying the outdoor paradise they live in.

Valdez is no exception. It's muddy, and there's not a lot of rhyme or reason to the way the town grew. It all seems a bit helter-skelter. Yet, there are those mountains, and the gorgeous bay on which the town sits. Given the setting, it's easy to forgive and forget any shortcomings.

On the way out of town, I drove past the little pond where I had seen the two trumpeter swans yesterday. They were still there, swimming in the part of the pond that wasn't iced over. For all I know, their swimming may contribute to pushing the ice away:

Nature's grace and beauty in full display

As I headed back toward Tok, where my Alaska leg of this adventure began, I drove alongside the Wrangell Mountains. Mountains in Alaska are so common, they can sometimes fade into the background of your consciousness. These stood out because of their sheer immensity.

Even hiding behind the clouds, this range is impressive

That's Mount Sanford, with an altitude of a bit over 16,000 feet. As a frame of reference, that's about 2,000 feet higher than Mount Rainier, which dominates much of the scenery of Western Washington. You can't see it in this shot, but off to the right of Mount Sanford is Mount Wrangell, which remains an active volcano. I grew up in the shadow of Mount St. Helens, though, and was there on May 18, 1980, when it blew its top, so I ain't afraid of no ghosts.

A few miles past the viewpoint for the Wrangell Mountains, I glimpsed, off to my left, a slight hint of movement. Turning the car around, I drove down a little dogleg, looking for whatever had attracted me out of the corner of my eye. It was another moose, feeding at the edge of a pond.

When I began posting pictures of wildlife on my blog during the trip, I got messages from people concerned that

I was either too close and risked being trampled, or that I was too close and would bother the animals. I took two photos as I left Valdez to show neither was the case.

First, here's a pretty typical shot I took of a moose, feeding, with two mallard ducks at its feet:

A typical wildlife shot, don't miss the ducks!

Then, here's essentially the same shot without the zoom:

The moose is the tiny dot on the horizon

Do you see the moose in that shot? It's the speck on the far shoreline of that frozen lake. I don't know how far away she was. Maybe 100 yards, possibly more? I'm terrible at visually estimating distances. What I know is, I wasn't close enough to the moose or ducks to bother them or be in any danger myself. Aside, that is, from the horrible little road that I had to put the Emerald Bullet down to get near that pond.

I arrived back in Tok in late afternoon and got a room at the same little place I stayed on the first night in Alaska. Tomorrow: Yukon, redux.

Day Eighteen

I felt more energized after a good night's sleep and got an early start from Tok, which was good because I ended up spending a decent portion of the morning birdwatching. I suppose "swan watching" is more accurate. I've never really cared about watching swans before, but I'd never seen them in the wild, and now I'm kind of hooked on them. I enjoyed watching them dive down for food, make nice with the other swans in the area, and even scratch themselves with their webbed feet, just like a dog.

I crossed the border into Canada before noon. I'd done three international crossings in the past few weeks, and they were not bad at all. The Canadian Customs man asked me a few basic questions and I gave straight answers, instead of being my typical smart-aleck self. I was through in less than five minutes, even with my incomplete paperwork. I'm sure he was able to check on my last two border crossings, and it all made a logical story. It also helps that there aren't a lot of people crossing the border at that location. There wasn't another car in sight when I cruised through.

About half a mile past the border, I pulled over to work whatever black magic was necessary so that I once again had Internet on my phone in Canada. When I glanced to my left, I spotted two more trumpeter swans swimming, with a third, looking kind of lonely, swimming by himself clear across the pond. I have pictures of those three, but I won't include them because I fear I am approaching the average person's tolerance for swan pictures.

I spent the rest of the day driving south-southeast on

a road I had driven north-northwest just a few weeks ago. Driving the same road in the opposite direction, I saw a lot of things I had missed the first time. Perspective is everything.

One thing I was noticing was that rivers and lakes that were frozen solid just two weeks ago were rapidly melting.

The Tanana River

Here's an example of what I mean about seeing things from a different perspective. I drove right by this dilapidated little cabin on the way to Alaska and didn't even give it a glance. Today, though, I was enchanted by it.

Just four more payments and it's ours

Why am I so attracted to old buildings that are falling apart? No idea. Maybe I love the idea that they could have just given up and fallen completely apart, but some element of pride keeps them standing as best they can. Perhaps I find comfort and self-realization in this. But I digress.

As I drove toward Haines Junction, I kept my eye peeled for wildlife, as always. I thought I saw a red fox scurry across a partially frozen pond, but by the time I stopped and backed up to look at it, there was no fox in sight. There were swans, though!

My last picture of swans, I promise

If this whole "being a writer" thing doesn't work out, I believe I've found my backup career: professional swan watcher. Any idea what the pay is for an entry-level swan watcher?

As the miles rolled under my wheels, I started to feel a little sentimental. I knew that the towering mountain ranges that had been my constant companions for the past two weeks would soon be only in my rearview mirror. I made myself feel better by constantly stopping and taking more pictures of them while they were still with me.

I'll miss them when I'm gone

I constantly try to keep myself open to what I call "happy accidents": times when I am looking for one thing, but stumble upon something even cooler, totally by accident. That happened this day.

I had stopped by the side of the road to take a photo of a tree that appeared to have a big hairdo on top. I took half a dozen shots of it, then drove off. Here's a small confession: my eyes are so bad that I can't actually see what I am taking a picture of. In the lens or on the screen of my camera, they all look completely fuzzy to me. It's not until I get to my room at night and upload them onto my laptop that I see what I've got, if anything. So, tonight, when I looked at the pictures of the hairdo tree, I was surprised to see I had captured another bird.

He could see me much better than I could see him

I arrived in Haines Junction in mid-afternoon, so I knew I could push on to Whitehorse before I stopped for the night. It was this area where I had first seen the incredible mountains that became my companions for the rest of my time in Yukon and Alaska. Turning east, I bid them a fond farewell.

I'll never forget these mountains

I made it to Whitehorse with no difficulty, and, turning off the Alaska Highway, I found there was a lot more to the town than I had originally seen on my first pass, when I zipped straight through. The capital of Yukon, it's got to be the biggest town on the Alaska Highway between Dawson Creek and the Alaska state line. I was too tired to find a place to eat, though, so it was the Magical Mystery Bag and a tiny little motel for me.

Day Nineteen

Before I started thinking about making this loop up to and around Alaska, I had never heard of the Stewart-Cassiar Highway. In fact, my plan was to take the AlCan its entire length up and back. Two weeks earlier, on my first morning in Alaska, as I was loading the Emerald Bullet for the day, a woman asked me if I had come up from the south. I said I had.

"AlCan?" she said.

I nodded.

She looked a little sad. "You missed a bet. I hope on your way back down, you'll turn south on Highway 37, just before you get to Watson Lake. You won't believe the wildlife you'll see."

I had immediately grabbed my map of western Canada, found Highway 37, and made a note. Today, as I left Whitehorse about 6 a.m., that was my plan—to hit the Stewart-Cassiar Highway and drive it all the way back to something that looked like civilization.

So, the first half of the day was spent once again backtracking over a road I had just driven, heading the other direction. I gassed up in the village of Teslin and took this shot of the Teslin Bridge, which I had photographed from high above two weeks ago.

Yes, I realize those are not real

Just a few miles past Teslin, I ran into a herd of caribou—the real deal this time, not statues:

The AlCan means caribou

Most of my shots of caribou show them running. That's because they are quite people-shy, and don't like me pointing something black at them, even if it is my Canon instead of a cannon. It was a caribou-centric morning for me, as I ran across another herd down the road.

My final caribou of this epic road trip

Shortly after that, I turned south on Highway 37, and my world changed. The Alaska Highway is a very nice road. It is broad, with nice shoulders in most places, which allows amateur photographers like me to pull over and get as many shots as I want. It's an easy, safe drive.

As soon as I turned onto the Stewart-Cassiar Highway, the wide-open vistas ringed by distant tall hills or mountains disappeared, to be replaced by dense forests of spruce and subalpine fir. It was lovely, but did leave me feeling closed in. The road itself mostly isn't bad, but it has two odd characteristics that make it less fun to drive: there is no center line, and virtually no shoulders.

When I see a semi barreling down on me from the other direction, my first instinct is to make sure I am well off the center line. (Should I say centre line? I *was* in Canada.) That's difficult to do when there isn't one—about all you can do is hug the shoulder, assuming there is one, but there isn't. Also, it rained the entire day, so it all added up to a slightly stressful, very muddy, drive.

After a few hours on 37, I pulled off at Boya Lake for a reprieve. Boya is very pretty. You can see from this photo that its ice was starting to melt. Around the edges, you can see the rocky bottom, but after just a few feet, it's ice the rest of the way:

Boya Lake, Yukon territory

Another note about the Stewart-Cassion Highway. From the time I turned off the AlCan, I never had a cellphone signal. I don't mean I had a poor signal; I mean I had a little "x" where the signal should be, a small "x" laughing at me, saying, "Oh, you thought you'd be able to call your wife out here? No, dear sir, no."

I thought that at least when I got to my hotel in Dease Lake, there would be some sort of cellphone coverage. This is proof that I am an optimist. There was none. The motel I stayed at claimed to have free wi-fi, but in a story as old as time, what they called wi-fi and what *I* call wi-fi were worlds apart. I would enter a website into my browser, go take a shower, have some dinner, read part of a book and come back to find it still loading.

Day one of driving the Stewart-Cassion Highway was a bit of a bust, especially as far as wildlife was concerned. I didn't see so much as a chipmunk. I did have a good experience staying at this small, privately owned motel in Dease Lake, though—especially when contrasted with the customer service at the Best Western in Valdez.

That service started early in the morning, before I even left Whitehorse. I laid my map out and tried to estimate how far I could make it, and what towns looked big enough that they might have a motel. I settled on Dease Lake, which actually had two motels to choose from—making it a major city by Stewart-Cassion standards.

It was still very early, but I took a chance and called one anyway. The phone rang only once before it was answered with a chipper and cheery, "Northway Motor Inn!" I didn't know anyone was that happy at 6:30 in the morning, especially when they were already at work.

"I'm coming in from Whitehorse tonight, and I'd like to make a reservation."

A small laugh from the other end. "We haven't been full, well, ever, I don't think. No need for a reservation, just come on down. When you see the service station, turn right, and we're right there. Oh, and if you're gonna be hungry when you get here, you need to make it to town by 8 o'clock. There's no restaurant in town, but the service station has a little deli where you can get a sandwich, but they close at 8."

I thanked her, hung up, and found myself pulling into Dease Lake a little after 7 p.m. I gassed up, since the station didn't open again until 8 the next morning, and I knew I'd be on the road long before that. I never would have known to do that if the helpful lady from Northway Motor Inn hadn't told me. After I got gas, I drove across the small side street to the motel.

When I walked in, the lady behind the counter said, "You look like a Shawn."

I guess they really weren't very crowded.

After I filled in the registration card, she said, "I've got a special room all ready for you, right here in the front, so you won't have to carry your bags so far. Oh, and I just baked these peanut butter cookies." She slid a plate of cookies across the counter. "You're not allergic to peanuts, are you?"

I told her I wasn't and plucked a warm cookie off the plate and made my way to my nearby room, feeling very contented and taken care of. It amazes me how much customer service can make a difference in a consumer experience.

The Best Western in Valdez was actually nicer than the Northway, but I'll go out of my way to stop here, if I ever again drive the Stewart-Cassion highway.

Day Twenty

When my eyes flew open at 4:55 a.m., my first thought was: I hope I see more animals today than I did yesterday.
Wish granted.

Just south of Dease Lake, I drove between two provincial parks—Mount Edziza Provincial Park and Stikine River Provincial Park, both in British Columbia. If you're wondering what a "provincial park" is, they are the loose equivalent of what a state park would be in the U.S. They are maintained by the province they are located in, as opposed to a national park maintained by the federal government.

My first sighting of the day actually completed my wildlife bingo card.

Bingo!

My first-ever bear sighting. It had such a sweet face that I almost convinced myself that it wouldn't dine on my innards if given the proper opportunity. It was a black bear, after all. About a week before I left on the trip, I had watched *Grizzly Man* with Dawn, and that was enough to keep me at a safe distance.

I drove five miles or so farther and saw another black bear, this time off to the left. He wanted no part of me, though, and disappeared before I could even grab a photo.

Just before noon, I had my greatest bear interaction. I saw this big fellow—only guessing at the sex by the size; if there's a way to tell the difference at a glance, I don't know what it is—rooting around in the undergrowth by the side of the road.

Mmmmm, grubs

This one looked at me, and our eyes met for a long moment. I was ready to jump back inside the safety of the Emerald Bullet, but then it went back to rooting around for lunch. I relaxed a bit and took about a hundred pictures of it.

The bear still was in no mood to move on, so I decided to share lunch hour with it: my one chance to say I'd eaten lunch with a real live black bear. I had a salami sandwich and chips. The bear, as far as I could tell, had roots or bugs. Finally, after a good half hour of communing with nature from the safety of my car, I continued on south.

This day wasn't just about bears, though, as nifty as that was. One other thing I always look for are large bird nests atop trees—always looking for an eagle's nest, I suppose. What I found, fifty more miles down the road, was this:

Definite winner of the stare-down contest

I am not familiar with most birds of British Columbia, and I had no idea what that was, so I asked in my blog and was told it was an osprey. That's cool enough, but it's the osprey's nickname that I like best. They are sometimes referred to as sea hawks, the kind-of namesake of my favorite football team.

A few minutes after 4 p.m., my cellphone woke from the

dead and began to beep and boop at me, scolding me for having dared to take it where there is no cell signal for almost 48 hours. Just like that, I knew civilization was on the horizon.

I try to avoid giving anyone unsolicited advice, but I'm going to break that rule this one time. If you ever find yourself in central British Columbia with a day or two to kill, I heartily recommend taking Highway 37, the Stewart-Cassion Highway, up to intersect the AlCan. It can be a bit of a lonely drive, and you will be cut off from many modern conveniences. But sometimes that's the point of a road trip, isn't it?

Day Twenty-One

Three weeks after leaving on my second mammoth road trip of the past year, I made it back to hearth and home, and the loving arms of my bride, Dawn Adele.

I'm not going to write much about this last day's travels. Too much of it was through towns and cities and freeways that seemed hopelessly congested and uncomfortable after my last few weeks of freedom from traffic, blaring horns, and one-finger salutes by road-raged individuals.

On the way down from the Canadian border to home, I decided to break my own rule and just go via the most direct route so I could get home at a decent hour. That meant a trip down I-5, through Everett, Seattle, and Tacoma. Blurgh.

Sitting in stopped traffic in Seattle, I so longed for the quiet of one of the little unnamed lakes I had sat beside, or the comfort of the towering mountains that surrounded me in the Matanuska Valley. In all the days I was gone, I hadn't seen a single person who seemed to be in a hurry. Everyone took the time to have a conversation with me, tell me a story, maybe share a laugh or two.

As I drove through the major metropolises of the Pacific Northwest, I saw tense shoulders on drivers leaning forward, looking for any advantage to cut an extra 30 seconds off their commute. I can't blame them—it wasn't that many years ago that I was one of those commuters, making that trek every day. I admit, though, it made me a little sad for them.

I pulled up to the house a little before 7 p.m. I had no more turned the key in the ignition than Dawn appeared on the front porch. She had been waiting for me, like a sea widow scanning the horizon.

Because I can never keep my mouth shut when I should, I said, "The last time I came home from Alaska, you bounded across the yard and into my arms." I didn't mention that had happened thirty-nine years ago, when we were both a bit younger.

Her answer? She turned around, went inside and shut the door.

Stupid Shawn.

Happily, she was waiting just inside for me, and, like she always does, she forgave me.

Home

Afterword

So often, as we get older, spontaneity disappears from our lives.

Here's what I mean. On September 1, 1982, I was sitting happily in the condo in Seattle that I shared with my oldest sister, Terri. I was parked in front of the television, watching MTV, which had premiered in Seattle just a few months before. Martha Quinn came on and gave a report on an upcoming music festival, called the US Festival, to be held in San Bernardino, California. She ran through a list of the bands that were going to be there, and it was tremendous: Fleetwood Mac, The Grateful Dead, The Police, The Ramones, Tom Petty and the Heartbreakers, Santana; the list went on and on. She signed off by saying, "It doesn't start for another 48 hours, so wherever you are in the United States, you've still got time to get here."

I'd had absolutely no plans to attend the festival, but the thought of all those best-loved bands playing on a single stage was too much for me. I walked into my bedroom, packed my backpack, and asked my sis for a ride to the airport. In less than a minute, I made the decision to shuck it all for a week and fly to Los Angeles, then bus over to San Bernardino.

Then, eventually, I grew up. I got a job where I couldn't just up and leave at a moment's notice. I became a responsible, functioning adult.

Until last summer. That was when I used my super-salesman powers of persuasion on my beautiful bride, Dawn Adele, and convinced her that we should once again shuck it all and head for the open road.

This trip to Alaska is a continuation, in many ways, of that same idea. Dawn and I had talked about making this

Alaska drive "someday." Then, I released *A Lap Around America* on the first of April, and it started to sell, and sell well. I knew I needed a follow-up to it as quickly as possible, so a drive to Alaska became more pressing.

It wasn't quite as spontaneous as grabbing my backpack and heading down to Southern California for the US Festival, but the whole trip came together in less than two weeks.

Once it was done, I felt reconnected with the state that has never left my heart or soul. I can't wait to go back again, the next time with Dawn at my side.

Because this trip was so much shorter than our Lap Around America, this book itself is shorter, too. I always try to give good value to my readers, so I am adding in two short memoirs that tell the story of what happened when I visited Alaska in the summers of 1974 and 1976. I hope you enjoy them.

My First Alaskan Summer

I almost threw away the best Christmas present of my life. I was thirteen years old in 1973, and as we did most years, my family opened presents on Christmas Eve at my Grandma Coleman's house in Centralia, Washington. We drove the back way from Mossyrock to Centralia so we could see all the Christmas lights.

The displays were simple compared to today, when there seems to be a house in every neighborhood with 20-foot-tall Santas, lighted nativity scenes, and tens of thousands of Christmas lights choreographed to music by the Trans-Siberian Orchestra. On our drive out town, we would just see houses with their rooflines defined by a single strand of multicolored bulbs. No matter; when I saw those lights, I knew Christmas had arrived.

At Grandma's house, she had pulled out all the stops. There was a dish of hard candy, a plate of cookies and a crystal dish with pickles and olives out on the table.

I had asked for only one thing for Christmas—an electric football game. The simpler technology of the day meant there were no realistic football games, but I had a friend with one of the electric football games, and so it was my heart's desire as well. Here's how it worked: each player would take several minutes to place their competitors in a complicated alignment, designed to stymie whatever plan their opponent had. When it was all set, you flipped a switch and the whole metal playing field vibrated, causing the little plastic men to jump around like over-caffeinated Mexican jumping beans. It was utter chaos. We loved it, and I was praying that one of the flat boxes under the tree contained one.

When the adults had finally had enough of playing their favorite game, called *Let's torture the kids by standing around talking instead of opening presents,* we got to the main event. As soon as my presents were set in front of me, I knew I had whiffed. There was nothing that looked like an electric football game. We were pretty poor that year, so my hopes hadn't been that high. I consoled myself by opening up a real football, two Hardy Boys books, some Hot Wheels I was a little too old for, then scarfing down one of Grandma Coleman's mincemeat cookies.

"Shawnie?" My mom. She and my oldest sister, Terri, were the only people on the planet to call me "Shawnie."

"Yeah?"

"I think you missed a present. I almost threw it away."

Those are about the sweetest words a kid can hear. With upturned eyebrows, I waded back into the ocean of wrapping paper, ribbon, and tape.

"What?"

Mom handed over a thin, flat package wrapped in red paper. "It's from Mickey."

My older brother was in Alaska, so we knew he wouldn't be here for Christmas. I hadn't expected anything from him, either.

I tore the paper open and saw there was a magazine inside. I was a nerdy kid, but even for me, a magazine seemed like an offbeat Christmas present. I flipped it over. It was the December issue of *Alaska* magazine. There was a picture of a river running in front of a mountain on the cover. I looked at Mom with an "I don't get it" expression on my face.

Mom had a suspiciously innocent expression on her face. She also looked surprised, but that was because she had drawn her eyebrows a little too high that morning. "Did you look inside and see if there's a card?"

I opened the cover, and, sure enough, there was a single piece of paper. I recognized Mick's handwriting immediately.

Shawn,

This magazine will have to take the place of your real present until you get out of school. Then, I'm going to send Mom

an airline ticket so you can come up and spend the summer with me. I've got a job as first mate on a ship called the Diver I. You can come and be a deckhand, too.
   Mick

My mouth had fallen open. I couldn't quite process everything. *Mickey is sending me an airplane ticket to fly to Alaska this summer?* Things like that didn't happen in our family. Did I mention we were poor? We didn't fly off to Alaska any more than the neighbors flew to Paris for lunch.

Two minutes earlier, I had been looking forward to heading home and reading my new Hardy Boys books. Now, all I could think about was Alaska.

Alaska. It seemed so far away, so mysterious, almost like a foreign country. June couldn't get there fast enough.

*****

In the '70s, summer vacation came earlier than it does today. We were free to drive our parents crazy as of the last week of May. I did exactly that, because I hadn't heard anything from Mickey. I still got my copy of the new *Alaska* magazine every other month, but they all came directly from the publisher—no notes from Mick telling me when I could come up.

Approximately 12,000 times per day, I asked Mom, "Have you heard from Mickey yet?" Or, "Do you know when I'm leaving yet?" Or, one of the dozen other ways that I had found to ask the same question.

After a week had passed, I begged Mom to call Mick and find out what the heck was going on. Was I even going anymore? We hadn't heard from him in months. Had he forgotten all about me?

"I know it's hard to wait, but we don't have any choice. Mickey's out on that boat, and there's no way to get ahold of him."

I knew this was true, but it didn't make the situation any more tolerable.

I said, "Unnh," which is early teenager for, *I am frustrated and have no words to express this sentiment.*

I went outside and found my dog, Sheba. When I didn't have the words, Sheba always understood me anyway. I grabbed her brush and sat on our side porch, brushing out clumps of hair. A white German shepherd, she shed her winter coats in chunks when summer arrived. I had become fascinated with this process and had started saving her fur as I brushed it off. I had a gallon jar stuffed completely full of Sheba hair. Yes, I was an odd kid.

I was pulling more tufts off her when Mom came down the stairs.

"Mickey just called."

I don't know how long she paused after those first three words. It felt like I aged several lifetimes, waiting to see what came next.

"I'm taking you up to the airport in two days. Your plane leaves first thing in the morning on Saturday."

I threw my arms into the air, giving myself the "Touchdown!" sign, then jumped straight up into the air. Sheba looked at me, tongue lolling, unmoved by my great good fortune. I hugged Mom, then picked up the jar of dog hair and took it to the garbage can at the back of the trailer. With a trip to Alaska on the horizon, how much hair Sheba would shed became a triviality no longer worth pursuing.

*****

I had flown once before, but it was on a little Cessna between Seattle and Bellingham. This flight to Anchorage was on a big jet. I was in that awkward twilight of childhood. I had started to think of myself as an adult, but I hadn't gotten my growth spurt yet, and my voice hadn't changed. Adults still treated me like I was a little kid. I was hoping that would change this summer. I envisioned getting on the airplane as a child and returning three months later as a strapping example of American manhood, possibly even with a full beard.

I had a window seat, and as we descended into Anchorage, we broke through the clouds. I saw mountain peaks poking up through white gauze. I took out my notebook and made a note. *Find out if that is snow or clouds covering the mountains.* Luckily, I never did ask anyone, and eventually figured out on my own that those were clouds, and there really wasn't thousands of feet of snowfall built up around Anchorage.

Mickey was waiting for me at the gate. That's how we did it in the '70s, before people came up with the idea to fly planes into buildings. He looked lean and strong, with a blue knit cap covering his already thinning hair, and an Irish-red beard. He hugged me. "You grew!"

I was still five foot two, just getting ready for the spurt that would shoot me past six feet tall. I smiled, unable to say anything. I was so thrilled to be in Alaska, I had temporarily lost the power of speech.

I wasn't sure what the weather would be like in Alaska in the summer, so I had brought everything from coats and sweaters to shorts and T-shirts. When we stepped out of the Anchorage airport, I was glad to find it felt warm, like a nice spring day back home.

"We're going to swing by and pick up some supplies, then driving back to Seward. We're heading out in two days."

"Heading out where?" I was just making conversation. I didn't care where we were going.

"Out into the Gulf of Alaska, then along the Aleutians."

I nodded. This all seemed very grown-up and exotic.

We ran through a grocery store, buying gallons of milk, loaves of bread, cans of soup and huge packages of meat.

"I suppose I should tell you, you're going to be working on this trip."

"Great! What am I going to be doing?"

"You'll help us on deck, when we bring the crab pots in, but you'll also be the chief cook and bottle washer."

I laughed. I knew that if I really concentrated, I could boil water, but that was the extent of my cooking ability.

"Don't worry. You'll be fine."

"I don't know how to cook."

"Here's the number one rule when it comes to cooking onboard: the first person to complain about the cooking, becomes the cook. I doubt if you'll hear a peep out of anybody."

As long as I don't kill them.

"Besides," he said, tipping me a wink, "I'll help you out."

I breathed a little easier.

I goggled at the scenery the whole drive back to Seward. I had always thought that Mossyrock was rural, but it looked civilized compared with Chugach National Forest. Mile after mile after mile of hills, mountains, trees and, even though it was June, a lot of snow-capped peaks.

We pulled into the Seward Harbor. Mickey pointed at a huge, ugly ship docked at the near end of the harbor.

"There's home."

I was a little skeptical. It was floating, but it looked like that could be subject to change at any moment. It had once been painted black but hadn't seen a new coat of paint in decades, and was now faded into almost a deep gray, with spots of rust scattered about.

Mickey noted my expression. "Doesn't look like much, does she?"

I scrunched my face up and shook my head.

"Don't worry, it's a lot worse when you get up close."

"Great!" I lugged my suitcase out of the backseat of the car.

Just then, a bearded man walked by, duffel bag slung over his shoulder. I looked down at Mom and Dad's suitcase and wished it was something cool like that. I knew that it marked me as a *cheechako*—a word Mickey had taught me on the drive that meant *newcomer*. Nothing to be done about it now, but I made a mental note for next summer.

The first thing I noticed about the harbor was the smell. It was overpowering. There was a fish and crab processing plant there, plus there was the general smell of creosote, saltwater, and tons of crab and fish coming and going, which all combined to create *eau de harbor*. It climbed up inside my nostrils and made me think I would never be able to un-smell it. I couldn't imagine living with that smell for the entire summer.

When we got to the *Diver I*, I noticed that Mickey was right. It did look a lot worse up close. There were no stairs from the dock to the ship. Mickey just walked right up to the edge of the dock, bags of groceries swinging from each hand, and jumped. He sat the bags on the deck, said, "Here, toss me your suitcase."

I did. Mick deftly plucked it out of the air, set it down, and picked up his bags. "Come on, I'll show you where you're gonna sleep."

He turned and looked at me, perched at the edge of the dock like a nervous parachutist.

He showed me his famous Mick smirk. "Yeah, we lost a guy last year, coming on board. He slipped and fell, then hit his head on the way down and drowned. He was drunk, though. You haven't been drinking today, have you?"

I cocked my head and gave him the closest thing I had to a dirty look.

Mickey laughed, then turned and walked away without a backwards glance. He had taught me to swim a decade earlier by throwing me into the deep water of Lake Mayfield, so I knew he wasn't coming back to help. The dock was steady, but the *Diver* was bobbing a bit with the waves. I gauged the distance, said a little prayer, and jumped. I landed safely onboard and immediately felt stupid for making a big deal out of it.

I followed Mickey's path and stepped inside the cabin on the main level. Straight ahead, there was a square dining table with a small lip all along the edge—designed to catch dishes in high seas. The kitchen was on my right. It wasn't much—a two-burner stove, a small refrigerator, an old chipped sink, and some cupboards.

Mickey was already putting the groceries away, and I saw why we hadn't bought a lot—there was nowhere to put them in the tiny kitchen.

"Okay, c'mon." He maneuvered around the table and showed me a room to the left.

"It's really supposed to be the captain's quarters, because it's right next to the wheelhouse, but Cap'n Bill doesn't want to be bothered if we're sinking, so he sleeps over there," he said, jerking his head at another door.

If this really was the captain's quarters, rank didn't mean a lot on board. It was the size of a closet. There was what passed for a bed—a piece of plywood with a thin mattress on it—that was smaller than a normal twin bed, and it took up almost the whole room. There was a door, though, so I was relieved that I would have at least a little bit of privacy that summer.

"Put your stuff away, then come find me."

There were two small drawers at the end of the bunk, so I put my clothes in those. I sat the comic books I had brought on the bed, and put my toothbrush, toothpaste, and comb under the tiny table beside the bed. I was unpacked.

I went back into the kitchen, but Mickey wasn't there. Instead, there was a young guy of maybe twenty years sitting at the table, eating a bowl of cereal. This is exactly what I had imagined it would be like to be a grown-up—eating cereal in the middle of the afternoon. He had blond, curly hair and wore a blue watch cap just like Mickey. Maybe it was part of the uniform.

"Oh, hey, you must be Mick's little brother. I'm Mike." He flashed a quick grin, then went back to his Alpha-Bits.

"Do you know where Mick went?" I made a mental note to call him that, instead of "Mickey." He was the first mate on board, so I didn't want to mess with his image.

"They're having trouble getting the motor to turn over, so he's down in the engine room. Go out that door and follow the stairs down."

I walked onto the foredeck and saw the huge stacks of crab pots. They were a lot bigger than I had anticipated. My family had gone crabbing at the ocean before, and the pots weren't much bigger than a TV tray. The ones on the *Diver I* stood about five feet tall and were broader across the bottom than they were the top. I couldn't imagine picking one up by myself.

I found the stairs and descended down into the darkness. The smell of oil was thick, and I saw an engine cover opened up. Tools and engine parts were scattered everywhere. Mick and an older man were standing, staring at it. Every other word of their conversation was a cuss word. There went my virgin ears.

After a moment, Mick saw me standing there. "Cap'n Bill, this is my little brother, Shawn."

The older man, balding and covered in grease, offered his hand with a smile. "Glad to have you on board. Mick says you're going to be our cook, too."

I smiled uncertainly. "Guess so, yeah."

"Don't worry, they'll be your biggest fans. We don't get too fancy. Mostly soup and sandwiches. This ain't the Ritz. If they don't like it, they can damn well cook for themselves."

I looked around the dank engine room and nodded my agreement.

"Hey," Mickey said, "did you meet Mike yet?"

I nodded again.

"He's getting the bait boxes ready. Go help him."

I didn't want to tell him that he was really up in the dining room eating cereal instead of filling the bait boxes, so I skedaddled up the stairs. I didn't know where the bait boxes were supposed to be, but I knew where I had last seen Mike.

I ran into the dining room and thought I'd missed him, but then I saw one work boot sticking out from the edge of the seats. I moved around and saw Mike, stretched out completely, his hat pulled down over his eyes. I was not about to wake him up.

Before I could leave, though, he said, "Whatcha need?" without moving the hat away from his eyes.

"Uhh ... Mick said you were filling the bait boxes, and he wanted me to help you."

"Correction," Mike said, finally pushing the cap away and squinting at the bright daylight, "I am *supposed* to be filling the bait boxes. It was a late night and an early morning. Come on, let's get to it."

I followed him down through the wheelhouse and down onto the deck. There was a metal table with white plastic boxes stacked on one side and a five-gallon bucket filled with, well, I wasn't sure what it was filled with, but it smelled absolutely awful.

"Here's all you do," Mike said. He popped the lid off one of the small boxes, scooped his hand down into the five-gallon bucket and came up with what looked like some part of a fish. He stuffed it into the bait box, snapped the lid back on, and picked up another. "It ain't brain surgery. That's all there is to it."

I'd been feeling a little queasy for a while, but seeing the fish parts all glopped together in the bucket, combined with the gentle rocking of the boat, made me think I was going to throw up. I didn't even know where the toilet was.

"I'll be right back," I said, running for the back of the boat.

I wanted to be anywhere that the bucket of chum was not. I leaned over the side of the boat, waiting to throw up, but it didn't come. After a few minutes, I walked back to the front of the boat.

Mike was still there, industriously slapping chum into the bait boxes, and smiling. He was singing the first two lines of the chorus of Bachman-Turner Overdrive's *Takin' Care of Business*, over and over. Never the third line, or a different verse. Just the first two lines. Over and over and over. I could see where that could lose its charm after a while, but I was hoping he would come up with a different song eventually.

He smiled at me in a way that told me that he knew I had been about to upchuck my cookies. "Don't worry about it. You ready to get started?"

I nodded weakly, took a pair of rubber gloves down off the metal table, and dunked my hand down into the chum bucket. I waited several moments to see if lunch was going to stay in place. It did, so I did just what Mike showed me.

There were over a hundred bait boxes to fill, but it didn't take too long to get them done. That was great, because I couldn't figure out which was worse—the smell of the rotting fish, or hearing the same few words of the BTO song over and over.

After half an hour or so, I needed to go to the bathroom.

"Hey, Mike. I need to pee. Where's the bathroom?"

"Follow me," he said, peeling his gloves off. He led me along the side of the ship to the back. There was a place where the railing had been cut away. There was a nail on the wall that had a roll of toilet paper on it.

"Here ya go."

I looked at the gap in the railing, then at the people that were walking by on the dock a few feet away.

"You're kidding, right?"

"No, man. The head quit working a few years back and it's never been fixed. We just whizz off the side of the boat."

"What if you're not just whizzing?"

He pointed to two handles fixed to either side of the railing. "Just hold on to those, hunker down, and do your business. We've got TP and everything." He said this as though he was saying, "And Cap'n Bill comes and puts a mint on your pillow every night."

I shook my head. The urge to pee was becoming overwhelming. "I don't think I can pee out here in the open, with people walking by."

"Yeah, I'm just shittin' ya, kid. Do you see that blue building over there?" He pointed at an oversized tin building fifty yards away. "That door on the left leads up to the Fisherman's Lounge. They've got showers and bathrooms there. Just go up the stairs."

Relief flooded through me. "Oh, awesome. Okay!" I stepped over onto the dock and began hurrying toward blessed relief.

As I did, I heard Mike shout, "But, when we're out to sea, this is really it. Get used to it!"

A problem for another day.

A few minutes later, I was back on the *Diver* and we were finishing filling up the last few bait boxes. Mick popped up from the engine room with a smile on his face. "I knew we'd get that old bitch running. Looks like we leave tomorrow. C'mon, I'll buy you dinner."

"Aren't I supposed to cook?" I asked, without a clue what that actually entailed.

"Time enough to punish everyone with your cooking in the days ahead. Come on, I'll buy you a burger and shake."

My stomach was still rumbly-tumbly enough that even a burger and shake didn't sound good, but after five minutes on solid ground, the feeling was gone. That wasn't necessarily a good thing. If I was getting seasick here, in port, with no chop at all, what would I feel like out on the open water? I pushed the thought out of my head. What were they going to do if I couldn't work, chop me up and put me in the bait boxes?

We drove into Seward proper. Seward wasn't a big town, just shy of 2,000 people in 1974. Growing up in a town of 400 had given me a different perspective, though, and Seward looked exotic to my eye, like something out of a movie set. There were almost twice as many men in Seward as there were women. Mickey said that automatically made every woman twice as attractive as she would have otherwise been.

I had nothing to compare that idea to. At fourteen, I wasn't just a virgin, I was a virgin who had never been on so much as a single date. One game of *Spin the Bottle* constituted my total experience with the fairer sex. That would not change on a ship filled with nothing but men, and I was good with that.

Women. Who needed 'em?

Mick parked in front of something called the Alaska Shop. I knew I'd found my Nirvana as soon as we walked in. The left side of the store was an old-fashioned soda fountain, with green countertops and red spinning stools. To the right of that was a wide selection of magazines, comics, and books. As if that wasn't enough, beside that was a huge selection of candy bars. I glanced beyond the candy and saw that there were a bunch of touristy displays and knickknacks, but I couldn't have cared less about a clock made out of a burl with a moose attached to it. Burgers, comics, and candy were my holy trinity, and they were all here, under one roof.

Mick and I had that burger and shake, then I spent twenty minutes rifling through the comics. I wasn't sure how long we were going to be at sea, but I figured it would be at least a few days. I would need Paydays, Reese's Cups, and Spider-Man to get me through, and I had a twenty-dollar bill burning a hole in my pocket.

My attention was captured by a red four-inch butterfly knife. It looked dangerous—exactly the kind of thing Mom would never let me buy in a million years.

Mick saw me looking at it and said to the clerk behind the counter, "Can we see the red butterfly?"

The clerk handed the knife to Mickey. He thumbed the clasp at the end, then flipped the knife out and locked it in place, all in one smooth motion. It was like a junior level switchblade. It was beautiful.

"How much?"

"Eight dollars."

"We'll take it." Mick looked at me. You'll have to buy your own comics and candy, but I'll buy the knife for you. If you cut yourself with it, don't come crying to me."

I had never loved my brother more.

I walked out of the Alaska Shop with a brown bag filled with goodies, a full stomach, and a smile on my face.

It was only when we climbed back in Mickey's car that I realized how tired I was.

"What time is it?"

Mickey glanced at his watch. "9:45. Why?"

My mouth fell open. "It's not even starting to get dark yet."

"It's summertime in the land of the midnight sun, boy. Get used to it."

On the drive back to the boat, I took the butterfly knife out and practiced whipping it open in a smooth motion like Mickey had. I did not achieve anything close to that, but I kept at it.

When we got back to the ship, I made the transfer from dock to ship a little smoother than I had the first time.

Getting this stuff down.

I was dead to the world, and all I wanted was to hit the hay. There was no actual bedding on my little bunk, but there was an old sleeping bag, and that worked fine for me. I stashed my candy bars under my bunk, stripped down to my tighty-whiteys, and crawled in. I was asleep almost instantly.

An indeterminate time later, I awoke with a start. There was still a pale light showing outside, but that didn't tell me much. I had this feeling of dread certainty that I was going to lose the burger, shake, and Payday candy bar I had devoured.

I threw open my door, bolted from my little room and made it to the side of the ship before I deposited my entire meal, and possibly my toenails, into the water.

I heaved and heaved, took a breath, then heaved some more. Finally, nothing but air was coming up, and I felt like it was safe to go back to bed.

Have you ever heard someone say they were so sick they wanted to die? I know when someone says that, they are not exaggerating. When it finally got mostly dark outside my window, I was praying for God to just come take me right then and there, because I knew dying would have to feel better than the nausea, which had somehow spread through my entire nervous system.

I lay in a cold pool of sweat for hours. Not long after it had gotten darkish, it started to get light. Finally, I fell asleep again out of sheer exhaustion.

What felt like ten minutes later, Mickey threw my door open. "Come on, sleepyhead! You've got five hungry guys waiting for breakfast." He took one look at my face, which I assumed was the color of the sea, and said, "Ah. Seasick. Okay. If you're lucky, it will pass. The good news is, I needed a part to get the engine running after all, so we'll be in port for another day before we take off. Don't worry, just lie here and close your eyes. Or, get up and do jumping jacks. It doesn't matter. You'll either get over it, or you won't. I'll go make breakfast."

He shut the door and I fell back to sleep.

I slept eight hours straight. When I opened my eyes, I braced for the wave of nausea to wash over me again. It didn't come. I swung my feet over the side of my bunk. My mouth tasted like

I'd been drinking water filtered through a cat's litterbox, and I had a slight headache, but the desire to find out whatever lay after this lifetime had passed. Somehow, while I slept, my body had made a magical adjustment.

I would never be seasick again.

I wandered out into the dining area to find everyone gathered there—Mickey, Cap'n Bill, Mike, and two other guys I hadn't met. One looked like a Native Alaskan, with dark skin and hair. The other had long, stringy blond hair and smirked at the sight of me.

"Hey, I'm Willy," the dark-haired guy said. He stood up and offered his hand across the table. I shook it with whatever strength I had left.

The long-haired guy gave me a nod, and said, "Hey, I'm Glenn."

I nodded back.

"You gonna survive?" Mickey asked.

"I think so. Just feel weak now."

"Well, we were just sitting here wondering who was gonna make dinner. Looks like that's you."

"Sure," I said.

I looked in the pantry. Thankfully, I noted some oversized cans of Campbell's Chicken Noodle Soup. I opened two of the big cans with the hand can opener, found a pan under the counter, and set it on the stove to warm up. I looked in the small fridge and found one of the packs of bologna we'd bought in Anchorage. I slapped that between two pieces of Wonder Bread, ladled the soup up and served it.

"Man. Best soup I've ever tasted. You've got a way with a can opener," Mike said.

"Yep. You're the best cook we've had since Bill fired the last guy," Willy said, smacking his lips.

Cap'n Bill winked at me. I wasn't going to get out of

cooking easily, I could see. My stomach wasn't ready for solid food yet, so I got a glass of water and took it outside. I noticed that the smell in the harbor wasn't as strong. Had it changed, or was my nose just adjusting?

A few minutes later, Mickey found me and laid a hand across my shoulder. "You gonna be all right?"

I gave a half-hearted smile and said, "I really think I am. It was weird. The boat was barely moving, but it felt like I couldn't get my balance. Now, I just feel like someone knocked the snot out of me."

"We got the part in that we needed today, so we're taking off tomorrow morning. Go get some more sleep, and we'll see how you're doing in the morning."

I was doing great in the morning. In fact, I woke up starving. Since I hadn't had any food that stayed down in 48 hours, that wasn't surprising.

I wandered into the galley looking to see who was up, but it was empty. I was tempted by the box of Lucky Charms I saw on the shelf, but I decided to do my best to take my job as cook seriously. I took a box of Bisquick down off the shelf and tried to make a batch of pancakes. I messed up the first batch of batter, but after I threw that away, I got it right. I found some bacon in the fridge, and put that on to cook.

I was entertaining illusions that I was a real cook when I realized that I had turned the burner up too high and the bacon was burned on one side and raw on the other. I was getting ready to trash that, too, when Cap'n Bill walked in.

"Oh, no. Never throw food away on board. Someone will eat it. Me, for instance." He grabbed the awful black/raw bacon and chomped down on it. He grimaced a bit, but powered through it. He poured himself a cup of what everyone called *ship's coffee* and grimaced again. Here's the recipe for ship's coffee: take a battered old coffeepot with no innards, shovel in five or six tablespoons of coffee, then fill to the brim with water and put on to boil. When it starts to boil, turn it down to a simmer and keep it there. As people drink it, keep adding more water and more grounds. Eventually, when a spoon will stand up in the pot, dump the whole mess out and start again. Yum.

I tried again, and managed to put a few pancakes and the rest of the bacon on the table, which was filling up quickly. I figured out that I needed to save a little of the batter and bacon for myself, because as soon as I put food on the table, it jumped onto someone's plate and disappeared.

I made second and third batches of batter and bacon, and eventually the guys started to drift away from the table to their chores. Finally, only Mickey was left.

"Get the dishes done, then come up to the wheelhouse. We're pushing off in just a few minutes. You're going to want to see this."

I made two last pancakes and scarfed them down dry as I washed the dishes. I ran up to the wheelhouse just as Mickey engaged the motor and we started to move away from the dock.

We moved toward what looked like a too-small opening in a rock wall ahead, but Mickey seemed calm, barely moving the captain's wheel. I stood in the open doorway and felt the wind on my face.

The closer we got to the opening in the breakwater, the more I saw it was plenty big. I had a lot to learn. As we passed through, I saw a bald eagle sitting on a post, staring off into the distance. We passed within ten feet of him.

Just like that, we were out in Resurrection Bay. Out in the open water, the boat moved a bit under my feet. I was so thankful I wasn't seasick any more.

"You want to take over?" Mickey asked with his sly grin.

"What? God no. Are you kidding?"

"Really, it's fine. Here, look." He spun the wheel to the left, stopped it, then back to the right. The ship kept going in the direction it had been all along. "It takes a long time to turn a boat this size. So, here's all you do. Do you see that point of land out there?" He pointed to a finger of land I could barely see, many miles away.

"Yes ..."

"Just point the nose of the ship straight toward it. If you're going a little to the left or right of it, just adjust the wheel a little bit. Eventually, you'll be heading toward it again. Got it?"

"Uhm, I guess so." I was two years away from even getting my learner's permit for driving a car. I hadn't expected to be driving a 107-foot boat. "How fast are we going, anyway?"

"The *Diver I* has a top speed of about eight knots. We're doing around six knots right now."

"How fast is that in mph?"

"Around seven miles per hour."

I laughed. "So, we could run faster than this boat."

"Have a little respect for this old boat. She's been to war. Now, she'll get us out and back safely. She always has. She's not a speedboat, she's a crabber."

Mick disappeared down below and I found myself all alone in the wheelhouse, captain of my own destiny. For the better part of an hour, I pointed toward the far distant point, watching it slowly drawing closer. Every time it felt like the nose of the ship wasn't pointed dead on, I made an adjustment.

Eventually, Mick came back into the wheelhouse, crooked his index finger at me, and said, "Come here, I want to show you something."

"Who's going to steer the ship?"

"No one." He grabbed me by the shoulder and led me to the walkway outside. He climbed a little ladder, until he was standing at the highest point on the ship. He waited until I clambered up after him.

"Look around. What do you see, as far as your eye can see?"

"Ocean?"

"Right. There's not much for us to run into out here. Now, look behind us. What do you see?"

I saw our wake, which was in a "Z" pattern. It looked like it had been made by a drunken toddler.

"When you steer a ship, you don't want to make a lot of little adjustments. Keep them smooth. Got it?"

I got it. I was a little deflated to realize that the important job I had been doing hadn't really needed me at all, but I didn't let that spoil my mood. I was standing on a ship moving through the Gulf of Alaska. The sky was deep blue, the water was calm, and there were dolphins playing alongside the ship.

Wait. What? Dolphins?

Yep, four dolphins were racing alongside us, jumping up and over each other. It was like being at SeaWorld for a show, but these guys were doing it for fun. It was one of the most amazing things I'd ever seen. I couldn't take my eyes off them.

"I didn't know there were dolphins this far north."

"Oh, yeah," Mickey said, as if it was old hat. "They love to play alongside the boat. You'll get used to it."

I doubted I would ever get used to seeing laughing, playing, sleek and shimmering dolphins playing tag with me.

I tore my eyes away. "What's next?"

"Next is, we'll put our first string of pots out. Then, we'll head to the next spot and drop our second string."

"How do we know where to put them down?"

"Bill knows. He's been crabbing since Moses was a toddler. Just listen to him, and you'll learn a lot."

I nodded. "Can I help put the pots out?"

"Yeah, but this first time, just stand back and watch. Everybody's got a job, and if you don't know what you're doing, you'll screw things up and somebody can get hurt. If you get hurt,

I know Mom will fly up here and kill me, so I don't want that to happen."

"Right," I said, but I had a hard time believing Mickey was really still afraid of Mom. What was she going to do, ground him?

A few minutes later, Cap'n Bill slowed the engines. I did as Mickey had told me, and stood at the back of the deck and watched Mickey, Willie, Mike, and Glenn drop the pots overboard. They were all connected by a thick rope, so when we brought them back up, hopefully loaded with crab, they would come one after the other.

When the last of the pots went over, it was followed by a buoy that would mark the exact spot, so we could find them again.

"How long do we have to leave them down there?" I had no idea whether it was a few hours, or a month.

"Not too long. A couple of days. That gives the crab plenty of time to crawl in to feed. Once they're in, they can't get back out."

While we moved to our next drop spot, I went back into the kitchen to fix lunch. I went back to my new best friend—soup and sandwiches. I took stock of the cans of soup and loaves of bread, and realized I'd be forced to try something more adventurous soon.

By early evening, we'd arrived at our second drop spot and laid out two long strings of pots, about ninety in all.

Mick took pity on me and cooked steaks for everybody for dinner. Everyone was glad to see something that didn't come out of a Campbell's soup can.

After dinner, I stood out on the front deck—much emptier now that the pots were sitting at the bottom of the sea. Cap'n Bill was piloting the ship to some cove where we would drop anchor for a day or two. The waiting part of crabbing had begun, and I was good with that. Everything had been happening quickly since my plane had landed.

Two hours later, we docked in a pristine little cove. I'd tell you the name of it, but I don't know if it's ever been named by anyone but me.

I took my butterfly knife out of my pocket and practiced opening and closing it. I was getting better. I stuck it down in the deck half a dozen times, just to see what would happen. I didn't sink the ship, which was good.

I retired to my cabin and read a comic book for a few minutes before I drifted off. It had been a good day.

When I woke up the next morning, Cap'n Bill told me that I didn't need to worry about making breakfast or lunch for everybody when we weren't actually working. "There's food here. If they starve to death, it's their own damn fault."

"Cap'n Bill, Mick didn't tell me how long we are going to be out this trip …"

"This is just a quick turnaround. Five or six days, then we'll be back in port."

Mickey had said I would get a half share of what the real hands got, so I was excited to get back with our hold full of crab to sell. I dreamed of all the good stuff I had seen in the Alaska Shop.

I killed most of the day sitting outside, reading my comics. I also had my first experience with using the outside toilet, which was nothing more than a space to hang your rear end out over the ocean. Probably the less said about that, the better. At least I didn't fall in.

In the evening, Mickey said, "Want to go on an adventure?"

I was fourteen years old. I *always* wanted to go on an adventure.

Mickey led me to the back of the boat, where a skiff dangled over the back of the *Diver*.

"Get in, let's go explore the cove."

The skiff was like a small rowboat, but it had a motor on the back, too.

As soon as we hit the water, Mickey fired it up and maneuvered us toward the shore. A mountain soared high overhead, with a glacier crawling across the bottom of it.

"You can't see it, but that glacier is moving. Constantly moving."

"How fast?"

"Not fast enough to run over us, don't worry. Look!" he said, pointing into the water beside the skiff. Two otters were swimming on their backs alongside us. They seemed to be smiling. They disappeared under the skiff and popped up on the other side. They swam with us all the way in to shore, then disappeared when we jumped out.

We walked along the shoreline a few hundred yards and stumbled on a new cove. This one was a little more hidden from where we were anchored. A flash of color beneath the water caught my eye. I walked to the water's edge and peered in.

The entire bottom of the cove was covered in starfish. They were all kinds of colors, and made the sea bottom look like a crazy kaleidoscope.

"Mickey, look! Have you ever seen that before?"

He shook his head. "No. Pretty cool."

I stood up straight, cleared my throat, and said, "I hereby declare this island to be Starfish Cove." My pronouncement probably would have carried more weight if my voice hadn't broken in the middle of it. Puberty is a bitch.

For a moment, I was lost in thought. I knew all my friends were back home in Mossyrock. They were hanging out together, maybe washing cars or mowing lawns for some extra money. Good enough. I was standing in the evening sunshine on the newly minted Starfish Cove, looking out at a rusting World War II vessel that was my new home. I'd seen a bald eagle, dolphins, otters, and starfish today. I knew I was the luckiest kid in the world.

We spent two days anchored off Starfish Cove. I'd read and reread all my comic books, so I went looking for something new to read. Cap'n Bill was lying on his bunk in his room. I knocked on the doorframe and said, "Cap'n Bill? Have you got anything to read?"

He pointed to a stack of magazines a foot tall at the end of his bunk. "If your brother doesn't care if you read them, you can have those. I've read 'em all."

I said "Thanks!" as I grabbed the stack and headed for my own bunk. I leafed through them. There were magazines called *True Detective, Front Page Detective,* and *Man's Magazine.* Most of them had women in distress on the cover. I wondered if it was possible they were in distress because they were only half dressed. I was hooked.

I lay down on my bunk, opened the first *True Detective* and was soon lost in a world of kidnappings, bad guys, heroic detectives, and true crime. The stories weren't nearly as lurid as the covers suggested, but that was okay; there were lots of good stories inside. Bill had so many of the magazines that, even as fast as I read, I couldn't get through them in the next two days.

On the third day, I woke to Mickey shaking my shoulder. "Come on, get up and make some breakfast for everybody. We've got a lot of work to do today."

"Okay, I will." I glanced outside. It was overcast, but light, which didn't tell me much. "What time is it?"

"4:45. We're gonna pull all the pots today, so we've gotta get an early start on it."

When I put my feet on the floor, I felt the rumbling of the engine below deck and realized we were already underway. This is crabbing: drop, kill time, and then hustle like hell.

I hurried into the kitchen and made the last of the pancake mix and sausages. If we picked up all the pots today, we'd be back in port in Seward sometime tomorrow. Might as well use what we've got.

By 7 a.m., everybody was fed and we spotted our buoy, right where it was supposed to be. Willie hooked onto it with a long pole, attached the rope to a winch, and started retrieving the pots. It's a pretty simple system. One at a time, a pot was brought up over the deck, dripping rivers of seawater and other muck from below. Mike would dash under the pot, release the netting, and everything inside the pot would tumble out onto the deck. We were after tanner crabs, which are much smaller than the king crabs often associated with Alaska crabbing. Tanner crabs weigh only a couple of pounds apiece, shell and all, as opposed to the red king crab, which can be several times that.

When the crab hit the deck, Mike, Willy, and Glenn all rushed in, grabbed up handfuls of crab and turned them over to look at the pattern on their underside. It was easy to differentiate the females from the males by their pattern. Females were tossed overboard; males went in the holding tank for delivery to the cannery. As soon as the pot was empty, one of the older guys would disconnect it and stack it in a corner of the deck.

I saw that if you just picked the crab up by the back it couldn't reach you with its pincers. By the time the third pot was emptied out, I was scampering after the pile of crab, sorting and tossing just like the other guys. I'm sure that after you've done it for twenty years it loses its appeal, but to me, it was just fun.

The weather was warm, the sea was calm, and every time I heard another crab splash into the holding tank, it felt like another quarter in my pocket.

It took us a few hours to empty the first string and stack all the pots, so as we chugged toward our second string, everyone was hungry again. I was starting to scrape the bottom of our supplies, but I managed to throw something together just as we got to our second buoy.

Cap'n Bill said, "Everybody down into the mess and grab

some grub, then we'll get these last pots and head for home. Glenn, you're on wheelhouse duty."

I set lunch out for everybody and took some up to Glenn in the wheelhouse. He had leaned back in the captain's chair, put his feed up, and closed his eyes. I set his lunch plate down and said, "Here ya go." He nodded, but didn't open his eyes.

I went down to the dining room and ate my own lunch. A few minutes later, I heard Bill say, "Goddamn it Glenn! You're supposed to be watching the buoy. Where is it?"

I'd never heard Cap'n Bill raise his voice before. I decided to make myself scarce. I left the galley and walked along the outer deck to the aft of the ship. Not too far behind us, I saw the apparent cause for concern—our buoy, bobbing safely behind us.

I went and found Mickey to tell him that I'd found the buoy, but he said he already knew.

"I'd go lay low for a little while. Glenn ran over the buoy while he was supposed to be on watch. I'm afraid Bill's gonna throw him off the ship right now."

I thought he was kidding about that last part, but I still went to my cabin and shut the door. My room was right next to the wheelhouse, so I could still hear Bill chewing Glenn out. I heard words used in combinations I'd never heard before.

"You shitdick little jackwagon fuckwaffle. Do you know what you've done? Now all our pots are sitting on the bottom, and we don't have fuckall idea of how to find them. I'm thinking of throwing you in with rocks tied to your ankles so you can locate them for us. Holy Moses on a pogo stick, you moron, get out of my sight."

I heard Glenn fly past my door, and I didn't blame him. I might have kept on until I got to the skiff, then headed for anywhere but here.

I cracked my door a little, and heard Bill and Mick talking.

Bill said, "We're in trouble. If I lose those pots, it's gonna bankrupt me. We've gotta find 'em, and I don't care how long we've got to stay out here. We're not heading back to port until I've got those pots."

"I hear ya, Skip. I've got an idea. Let me go to work on it."

My brother. He always had ideas.

After a few minutes, it felt safe to come out, and I found Mick on the front deck, attaching a grappling hook to a long rope that was looped on the deck.

"Cap'n Bill thinks we're screwed, but he didn't count on the genius of me."

Modesty runs in my family.

"Here, help me get this rope aft. We're gonna trawl for the pots."

I helped carry the long rope to the back of the boat. Mick tied one end to the back railing, in a fancy knot I couldn't have replicated in a thousand years. He took the end with the grappling hook and dropped it overboard. He fed rope out until he felt slack and knew the hook was on the bottom.

"Okay, we can't be too far from where shit for brains fell asleep and ran over the buoy. Go tell Bill we're ready, and he'll start trawling.

I found Bill in the wheelhouse and passed the message on from Mick. He nodded, started the engine and we moved forward, very slowly. I guessed "trawling" meant "going very slow."

I ran back to the back of the boat and watched Mickey watch the rope. I had a lot of questions, like, "How can you tell if it's still on the bottom?" and "How will you know when you've got something?" but I sensed this was not the time to be asking a lot of little-kid questions.

After a while, I got bored and climbed up the ladder to the highest level. This was my favorite spot on the ship. I felt like I could see forever. I figured Mickey would hook the pots in no time, and we'd be on our way home.

I was very wrong.

We trawled until close to midnight, then Bill put us into the nearest cove, and we anchored for the night.

Bright and early the next morning, we were underway again. Overnight, Mickey and Bill had taken a map, circled an area, and were slowly drawing black lines, both horizontally and vertically, which I guessed represented areas that we had already trawled.

The good news was that no one was asking me to cook. The bad news was, that was because we were running very low on supplies. We'd eaten the last of the meat the night before. All the milk and juice was gone, and we were down to whatever water was in the holding tank to drink.

So, what did we eat? We ate what we had on board—crab. Over the next week, we ran out of everything but crab, so we cooked that every way we could think, which I'll admit was pretty limited.

My problem was, I didn't like crab in the first place. After having it more than a dozen meals in a row, I had grown to hate it.

On the fifth night, as we were anchored alongside a nearby island, another, smaller boat pulled alongside. Across the short expanse of water, we told them our tale of woe. They offered to trade us some of their scallops for some of our crab. We gladly took them up on it. Mickey cooked the scallops. When supplies are low, you don't put the last of them in the hands of a fourteen-year-old who doesn't know a pot from a hole in the ground. They were delicious, mostly because they weren't crab.

Ten days into our trawling adventure, we got more bad news. The pump that moved fresh seawater into the hold stopped working. Without fresh water circulating, the crab we already had would die, and the whole trip would be a disaster.

Mickey and Bill went to work on the pump, but there was nothing they could do. We turned tail and ran back for Seward, hoping to get back in time to rescue what we already had.

It was late by the time we pulled into port. Everyone scrambled into position as Bill steered the ship into position. Bill hadn't even killed the engines before Glenn had his duffel slung over his shoulder and jumped onto dry land. He lit out for town. I never saw him again.

The next morning, we found out that every crab in the hold was dead. It really was a disaster for Bill. He had lost half his pots and didn't have the cash to replace them. The crab that might have paid for new ones had to be dumped.

The crew had it rough, too. Glenn deserved to be thrown off the ship. He had slacked off and caused everyone else a lot of heartache. Mickey, Willie, and Mike had worked their butts off for two weeks and they had nothing to show for it. It was a bad bit of business all the way around. I suppose it was bad for me, too, but the money I thought I might earn on the voyage had never seemed real. I was living a dream, being out on the water, spending time with my brother, seeing things I might never have seen in a lifetime, so any money would have been nice, but it wasn't necessary for me.

The day after we tied up in Seward again, everyone but Mickey and I scattered. Cap'n Bill had a girlfriend up in Wasilla, and he went there to drown his sorrows with her. I have no idea where Mike and Willie went. Caught on with other boats that weren't as snake-bitten as the *Diver I*, probably.

Since we were back in port, we could at least go to the grocery store and restock the essentials—meat, milk, cereal, and comic books. Okay, that last was probably just an essential for me.

There was no entertainment on board the ship, but Mickey pulled out a scrimshawed cribbage board. I'd never played cribbage. It had always seemed like an adult game, like pinochle.

"Here. We'll play a few hands with our cards face up. You'll get the hang of it."

I took to it pretty well, but it took me two days of begging Mickey for one more game before I actually beat him.

The Fisherman's Lounge at the cannery was nice, too. They had showers there, which I didn't feel like I needed, but Mickey insisted. There was also a big open room with a few couches and easy chairs, with magazines and books scattered around. There was even a television in the corner that didn't come in very well, but I was a teenager, and I'd watch anything, even if it was snowy and rolled every once in a while.

While I goofed off, doing a whole lot of nothing, Mickey worked around the boat, keeping himself busy. One day, when I came back on board from a visit to the Fisherman's Lounge, he said, "Got the pump in the tanks working."

He led me over to the huge empty tanks, and sure enough, I could hear the hum of the pump as it circulated the water.

"Too little, too late, but if Bill ever takes her out again, at least it will be running."

If I'd been Mickey, I might have been worried about where my next meal was coming from, but he didn't seem to think about it. For the time being, we had our own little floating hotel to live on, and that was good with us.

One morning, after breakfast, Mickey said, "C'mon. Let's go."

"Let's go where?"

"Somewhere. Anywhere," he said, grabbing the binocular case off the nail by the door. "We've been stuck on this boat too long. Let's go."

I really hadn't minded being stuck on the boat. I couldn't smell the overwhelming odor I'd first noticed, and life was pretty mellow with just the two of us hanging out. We played a lot of cribbage and read a lot of books. Still, an adventure was always good.

We climbed into Mickey's car and when we pulled up to the highway, there were cars streaming into Seward.

"What the heck is going on? Where did all these cars come from?"

"It's the Fourth of July, dummy. Didn't you know that?"

"Heck, I don't even know what day of the week it is." I enjoyed being completely free of the calendar. There would be time enough for that when I went home and had to start my freshman year in high school.

"Okay, so it's the Fourth of July. Why is everyone coming to Seward?"

Mickey shook his head at my ignorance, but he was smiling. "Today is the Mount Marathon race. People come from all over the state to watch these fools crawl up a mountain, then jump back down it."

"Oh, I see," I said, as though I understood, when I really didn't understand what he was talking about at all.

"You'll see. First let's see if we can fight our way through the crowds at the café and get something to eat. I'm tired of eating my own cooking and not crazy enough to eat yours again if I don't have to."

"Good plan."

Overnight, Seward had erupted from a sedate town of a few thousand people to a boomtown with many times that. They all seemed to be out on the sidewalks, walking, gawking, and talking.

We finally managed to find a place with a table open and grabbed a quick lunch. After he paid, Mickey said, "Come on. I've got a great place to watch the race."

We walked the main street, passed a banner that hung over the road that read. "Mount Marathon Race, 1974."

"It's like this race is famous, but I've never heard of it."

"It's famous in Alaska, but people in the Lower 48 don't

know about it. I think everyone around here would like to keep it that way, but it won't last. Everything gets discovered eventually, everything gets ruined."

I was too young to have properly developed my cynicism, but I nodded seriously, as though I understood and agreed.

We turned left up a side street and walked a few blocks toward the trail that led up to Mount Marathon.

"So, as a cheechako, what do I need to know about the race?"

"Let's see ... the whole damned thing started more than fifty years ago, as a bar bet. That's how most good things get started, you know—two drunk guys making a bet. Anyway, they bet whether or not someone could run to the top and back down in less than an hour."

"Do they?"

"Yeah, some do, every year. I think the record's about 45 minutes. But, here's the interesting thing. It takes more than half an hour to get to the top, and just a few minutes to get to the bottom. Craziest damn thing you'll ever see. They say that if you aren't bleeding by the time you get to the finish line, then you weren't trying very hard."

Now I was enthralled. Athletic competition and blood. What could be better?

"Here. Take the binoculars and look up and down the mountain. You'll be able to see the trail they climb."

I took the binoculars, adjusted them, and located the trail, which seemed to go straight up the mountain. "Holy cow! It goes straight up! No switchbacks?"

Mickey gave me his, 'Are you kidding?' look and said, "This is Alaska, son. No need for switchbacks that just slow you down. We go straight up, because we're tougher."

Looking at the trail, which looked to be at about a 45-degree angle, I could only agree.

We heard a stampede of feet slapping the pavement and turned to see the herd of runners. There were hundreds of them coming, but a few were already distancing themselves from the pack. So far, so good—it looked like any other race. Soon enough, though, the runners left the city street and hit the trail. They disappeared at the bottom of the mountain, which is ringed in greenery, then reappeared farther up, where there are cliffs and rocks. The top third of the mountain looked like nothing but shale.

When they hit the steep trail up, the race slowed to a crawl. When I focused the binoculars on them, I could see they were moving, but every step looked painful.

"Have you ever climbed up there?"

"Yeah, of course," Mick said, as though he did it every day.

"Can we go?"

"Sure. We'll let the Fourth of July crowds die down, then we'll go in a few days."

"Cool," I said, and fitted the binoculars against my eyes again. There was something hypnotic about watching the racers, who were no longer runners, climbing up the side of the mountain. After a few minutes, there was an entire string of racers climbing.

"How tall is it?"

"Just a little over 3,000 feet tall. It's not the height that does it, it's how steep it is, and how fast you gain elevation."

I watched as the climbers at the head of the line reached the turnaround point at the top. The slow, steady ascent changed into a running, jumping descent. They often jumped out of my ability to keep track of them with the binoculars.

Just a few minutes later, the first runner emerged alone, flying down the street. He was indeed bloodied over the lower half of his body.

"Cool …" I said to Mick. He just smiled at me. He was close

enough to being a teenager himself to remember what teenage boys liked.

Less than a week later, we set out to do the climb ourselves. As I started up the nearly vertical section of the mountain, I was fourteen years old, weighed less than 120 pounds and, coming out of basketball season, was still in good shape. I recalled those climbers who I had thought looked so slow. After two minutes, my lungs were tearing out of my chest.

I collapsed and said to Mick, "Please, get me an oxygen tent. Are we there yet?"

Mick was huffing and puffing and looked a little red in the face, but he was trying not to show that he, too, was already near death. He had apparently lost the power of speech, but he did manage to point toward the top. I craned my neck and looked. It looked as far away as my hope of a soft bed.

Finally, with a concerted effort, he said, "You wanna give up?"

Of course I wanted to give up. We could have easily been back on the *Diver I*, playing cribbage, drinking a Pepsi and relaxing. Instead, my lungs were on fire.

I shook my head. "No. You?" I said a silent prayer he did.

He didn't answer, but turned and started slowly moving up the mountain. Damn.

Where the Fourth of July racers had just plugged constantly along, Mick and I stopped and rested. A lot. Each time our hearts felt like they might actually explode out of our chests, we would find a companionable piece of dirt or shale to sit on and lament that we had ever tried this foolhardy exercise to begin with.

Finally, almost three hours after we started, we summited Mount Marathon. At fourteen, I hadn't set that many goals for myself to achieve, but I knew I had this going for me. For the rest of my life, I could say that I had climbed to the very top of Mount Marathon. The pain of the ascent started to fade into the background almost immediately—the benefit of being a teenager, I suppose.

We sat for a few minutes and looked at one of the most incredible views in the world—the Seward Mountains, extending to our left and right, and Resurrection Bay far below us, a crystal blue mirror, with more mountains beyond that. We could see Seward Harbor and even managed to pick out the *Diver I*.

Then, without warning, Mick stood, dusted the butt of his jeans off, and set off down the mountain at a fast clip. "See you at the bottom, slowpoke," he said over his shoulder.

I sat there, shocked into immobility. What a cheater! I was having none of that.

I launched myself from my sitting position and took off. I had thought that going down would be a piece of cake after the torturous climb, but I soon learned that it just punished a different set of muscles. No matter, I was intent on catching up to the white T-shirt I could see bobbing twenty yards in front of me.

I had always idolized Mick. Being ten years older than me, he always seemed to set an impossible standard for me to meet. I felt like I would never be as good at anything as he was at everything. Except, maybe, descending Mount Marathon.

I moved from a jog, to a lope, to small jumps, to bigger jumps. The loose shale skittered dangerously around my tennis shoes with each landing, but I ignored it. I couldn't believe I was actually catching up to Mick.

A few moments later, I was even with him. Triumph surged through me. "Ha, ha, ha, ha! See ya, old man!"

"Shawn, wait! Slow down."

"No way! Catch me if you can, old timer!"

Those few moments of triumph were sweet, but ever so short. Almost instantly, I got this sickening feeling in the pit of my stomach that I had lost the ability to slow down, or even to maintain the same speed. My jumps turned to a run as I struggled to keep my balance. The pitch of the mountain gave me no chance. It wasn't even close. One moment, I was an upright antelope, leaping down the side of the mountain. The next, I was a dislodged tumbleweed, spinning head over heels, any whisper of control long since gone.

I saw blue sky, brown shale, blue sky, brown shale, over and over and over. I lost count of how many times I rolled down the side of the mountain. After an eternity of bouncing, falling, tangling, and slamming my slim body against rock, I came to rest face-down.

My right arm was buried underneath me. It felt like my legs had somehow disengaged themselves from my body and kicked my own ass, repeatedly. If I was a younger kid, I'm sure I would have burst out in tears. I was a young man, though, so I just said a string of very bad words while my eyes leaked profusely, sending streaks down my face, ravaged from scraping the last five yards or so in flinty shale.

Mick was there in a moment, panic etched across his face. "Shawn. Shawn. Are you okay? What the hell were you thinking, going that fast?"

I couldn't manage to answer, but I did manage to pull my right hand out from under me. It felt numb. I looked down at my hand. The thumb was pointing backwards at an unnatural angle. All the skin on the outside of the arm, from my elbow to my wrist, was gone.

Every part of me hurt.

Mick's eyes grew large when he saw my hand.

"Let's just sit here for a minute and rest," Mick said. "Then we'll figure out what to do."

I blinked away the dirt and tears from my eyes and saw that we still had a long way to go. "There's nothing for us to do, except climb down. What are we gonna do, have an ambulance drive up the side of the mountain?"

Mickey nodded, put his arm around my shoulders and pulled me close to him. "Stupid, crazy kid," he said softly.

I felt like shock was setting in, so after a minute, I said, "Come on, let's go."

I didn't actually believe I could do it, that climb down, when I hurt so bad.

You know what, though? When there are no good alternatives, a horrible choice becomes your only choice.

I have no sense of how long it took us to hobble the rest of the way down the mountain, me leaning on Mick and using him like a crutch, with my good left arm around his shoulders. It might have been an hour, or it might have been several weeks. It seemed like the latter.

At the bottom, Mick helped me into his car, and then drove us back to the harbor. Instead of going to the doctor, or back to the *Diver I*, he drove us to the Fisherman's Lounge. He helped me up the stairs, which I needed, because my legs had pretty well given out.

I took a hot shower, which felt like heaven on my quivering muscles and like hell on my many open wounds. When I came out, Mick had retrieved the first-aid kit from the ship and bandaged up the worst of my scrapes and contusions.

He looked at my right thumb. "That just don't look right."

I agreed.

"Move it for me."

I nodded and tried to move my thumb. It moved the same way the statue of David might move its thumb, which is to say, not at all.

I never saw a doctor. I didn't need one for the scrapes and bruises. Those all healed on their own. I have no idea what I did to my thumb, though, because it remained frozen like that for about eighteen months. I had to learn a new way to hold a pen or pencil, because I couldn't grip it between my thumb and forefinger. Eventually, sitting in class one day in the middle of my sophomore year, the thumb twitched and came back to life.

I limped around the harbor for the next few days, but aside from my paralyzed thumb, I hadn't really sustained any damage, and I came away with a bitchin' story to tell for the rest of my life.

While my body healed, we continued to do a whole bunch of nothing. Apparently, Cap'n Bill, disgusted at losing half his pots, had retreated semi-permanently to Wasilla. Mick took me back to the Alaska Shop and let me pick out whatever books I wanted to read. I chose one called *The Last Catholic in America*, by John Powers, because I read the first page and knew it was going to be hilarious. Mickey bought *All Creatures Great and Small* by James Herriott. We each burned through our own, then swapped and hustled through each other's.

About two weeks after my tumble down the mountain, while we were in town, Mick suggested we call Mom. I felt an odd sensation right then. I had been away from home about six weeks at the time, but hadn't really thought of what was going on in Mossyrock. There was too much going on in Alaska to worry about that.

But, as soon as Mick mentioned calling home, I felt a terrible wave of homesickness. Out of the blue, I missed my dog, Sheba, my room, with my comic book collection, the cherry tree I used to climb up every day in the summer to read. I even missed my mom and step-dad a little.

Mick found a payphone, dialed the number, and dropped a bunch of quarters in. I could hear the ringing through the earpiece, and somehow even that made me homesick.

When Mom answered, Mick said, "Hey, just a minute," then handed the phone to me.

"Hello?" I hated that my voice sounded a little shaky.

"Hi, honey. You ready to come home?"

No, I thought. Of course I'm not. I never know what I'll see up here. It might be a moose, or a bear, or a bald eagle, or we might go climb a mountain. We might go out on a boat and nearly starve because someone literally fell asleep at the wheel. Back home, there were lawns to be mowed, school clothes to be bought, garbage to be taken out. Mundane stuff. Of course I wasn't ready to go home.

I was dismayed, then, to hear my own voice say, "Yes."

Mick looked a little surprised at first, but then he twitched the corner of his mouth in a gesture that told me he remembered what it was like to be a little homesick, too.

I don't remember the blur of the rest of that conversation, but soon enough, I handed the phone back to Mick and he and Mom made the arrangements for my flight home.

Mick and I drove back to the boat in silence. I felt like I had betrayed him. He had sent for me, paid for me to come, and watched out for me all summer, and I repaid him by deserting him the first chance I got.

When we got back to the boat, Mick took down two bowls from the cupboard, poured us both a bowl of cereal, and said, "Well, did you have a good time here, this summer?"

"The best," I told him, and it was true.

"Good. Want to come back next summer?"

"Yes!"

"Good," he nodded. "Go get the cribbage board. Let's play."

A quick thought on these two memoirs. When I write true stories, I have a specific process to aid in creativity. I listen to an endless loop of the music I listened to during the time I'm writing about. I look at any old pictures I can find from that time. If possible, I talk to other people who were there with me. I do everything I can to put myself back into the same frame of mind I was in at the time. Instead of being a middle aged man writing about a young boy, I try to capture what my thoughts and voice were like at the time.

Only two years elapsed between the events of *My First Alaska Summer* and those of *My Matanuska Summer*. However, reading them back to back, I can see what great changes had come over me in just twenty-four months. At fourteen, I was much more child than man. At sixteen, I lacked any discernible sign of maturity, yes, but I was grappling with much more difficult issues the second summer. At fourteen, my only moral dilemma was whether or not to read Cap'n Bill's slightly racy magazines, which I succumbed to pretty easily. Two years later, the things I was confronted with were more important.

Did I want to partake in drugs or alcohol? They were certainly available to me if I wanted.

Did I want to work a nice, steady, if somewhat boring job painting apartments, or did I want to be a part of one of my brother's crazy schemes. How about gambling? Was I ready for that?

I'm no saint. I sailed through some of those waters untouched, and gave in to temptation at other times. Which was which?

The answers are next, in *My Matanuska Summer*.

My Matanuska Summer

"Here ya go," Bobby squeaked, sounding like a burst of helium from a balloon. He held the joint out. Smoke curled from the tip, beckoning me.

I knew this moment would arrive. Just didn't know it would be right this second. What do I do? Uhh…

It was June 10, 1976. I was sixteen years old, sitting at the end of a tatty L-shaped sectional in my older brother Mickey's apartment in Seward, Alaska. My plane had touched down from Seattle less than five hours earlier. I was not ready to face an unexpected life decision.

Time slowed. Four older guys sat around the couch, looking at me with mild curiosity.

The decision weighed on me more than for most. Five years earlier, seeing what addiction had done to the rest of my family, I had decided never to take that first drink. *If I never have a first drink,* I had thought, *I'll never become an alcoholic.* As the years passed, that vow had gone unchallenged. I was a nerdy kid who didn't get invited to parties, and the friends I hung out with didn't drink or smoke either. Easy, right?

Not being tested by peer pressure had its downside. I didn't know if I was firm in this lifelong decision. I hadn't yet been faced with a smoldering joint a foot and a half from my face.

Said joint wavered a bit in the air, sending a genie of smoke toward my nostrils. It smelled a little skunky, but it had a certain beckoning appeal.

So did a life without addiction.

I grinned, shook my head. "No thanks. I don't smoke."

Bobby shrugged, blew lungfuls of smoke upward to join the hazy cloud near the ceiling. He passed the joint back to his right, and with that, I knew I meant what I had vowed and believed. I was never going to smoke or drink.

None of the guys slouching around the couch cared either way. The peer pressure I had seen on *After School Specials* was absent.

One of the four guys on the couch was my brother Mick. He was ten years older, a few inches shorter than me, with a full Irish red beard and a hairline already moving the wrong direction. He accepted the joint, took a drag, then passed it on. "Figured since you were sixteen now, you might have started smoking."

"Nope."

"I won't have to worry about you raiding my stash, then, right?"

"For sure."

After an evening of stoned conversation, smoke, and munchies, the apartment cleared out. That left just me, Mick, and his wife Joann. I don't know how thrilled Joann was to have her new husband's teenage brother staying with her for an indeterminate period, but so far she appeared to be a good sport about it.

Mickey deftly rolled a new joint, then leaned back against the cushions. "So, what do you want to do this summer?"

I'd like to meet a girl, but that's probably not going to happen. "I don't know. Maybe get a job? I need to make some money for school clothes, and I really want to buy a car. I'm sick of riding the bus."

Mick nodded. Mom had bought him a brand new '65 Mustang fastback when he was sixteen. We both knew she wouldn't make that mistake again.

"I can hook you up. I do odd jobs for the guy that owns this building. He owns a bunch of apartments in town, so people are always moving in and out. He needs someone to get them ready for the new tenants. How does that sound?"

That sounds like a lot of cleaning up after other people. It also sounds like being stuck inside a series of crappy little apartments all summer.

It sounds like school clothes, and perhaps a car. "Sure. Sounds good."

"He pays five bucks an hour, under the table."

That actually did sound good. Minimum wage was $2.30, so raking in double that amount, with no work experience of any kind, was more than I had any right to expect.

I spent the month leading up to the Bicentennial celebration painting tiny apartments' walls an avocado green color. After three weeks or so, that institutional green colored my dreams as well as every waking moment. I had made a couple hundred dollars, but between my comic book and candy bar habit, there was no way I was going to earn enough to buy a car when I got home.

Shortly after July 4th, Mick sat me down and proposed a new adventure. We were sitting around that same L-shaped couch, this time eating mac and cheese and listening to *The Lovin' Spoonful's Greatest Hits* on the stereo.

"Are you liking painting apartments?"

I shrugged.

"Well, I've got something new coming up, and if you want, you can be a part of it."

My brother. As long as I had known him, he had "something new, something big" coming up. I couldn't remember any of those things ever working out. Still, he paid for me to come to Alaska every summer. I owed him a lot just for getting me out of Mossyrock three months out of every year.

"What?"

"Before I tell you, you've got to promise to keep it under your hat. If you tell Mom what I'm about to tell you, she'll never let you come up here again."

I nodded. *Keep something from Mom? I've got that skill down pat already.*

"What is it?"

"I'm going to go camp out up in the Matanuska Valley. It's a place that I've got scouted out. "

Mick and I had gone for drives up through the back roads of the Matanuska Valley. It was gorgeous. It was also the kind of place where you could drive for many miles and never see another human being.

"Scouted out for what?"

"I'm going to do a little grow operation. The Matanuska Valley is one of the best places on earth to grow crops. Twenty hours of summer sunshine every day, incredible soil, perfect growing conditions."

I didn't need to ask what kind of agriculture Mick had in mind. At the time, there were basically four types of marijuana: Acapulco Gold, Maui Wowie, Matanuska Thunderfuck, and locally grown skunk weed, which was often passed off as one of the other three. I'm sure there were other variations, but that was most of what we saw in Mossyrock.

"You gonna stay up there, or go back and forth?"

"Once the plants are in the ground, I'm not leaving. Gotta keep an eye on them."

"How long are you going to be gone?"

"About six weeks. I've been saving seeds all year and I started 'em in a greenhouse a few weeks ago. I've just got to get up there and put 'em in the ground. You want to help me?" He took a bite of mac and cheese, which gave me a moment to think.

I had $160 stashed away from painting apartments. Enough to buy my school clothes, probably, but nothing else. "Maybe."

"I know you're wanting to buy a car. I remember being your age." Mick leaned back, put his feet up. "Listen. If you want to stay here and keep painting apartments, you can probably go home with what, five or six hundred dollars?"

"Yeah. Probably." *Not to mention a lifetime aversion to babyshit green paint.*

"I can't be sure, of course, but I think this crop is going to net me about ten grand or so."

"Maybe," Joann chimed in from the kitchen. She was already learning not to count on his big plans.

Mick grimaced at the kitchen, looked at me and shook his head. "If you want to come camp with me, and if you work your butt off, I'll cut you in for ten percent."

Easy math. Stay in town, living with my brother's wife that I don't really know and make a sure six hundred dollars, or go spend the summer camping with my brother, maybe make a grand.

"I'm in."

*****

Early the next morning, we loaded up The Bumblebee and drove north from Seward. The Bumblebee was Mick's yellow-and-black-striped 1970 Toyota Corona. You might think that two enterprising young dope growers would have a huge van with blacked-out windows, or at least a big pickup truck loaded with equipment, but not us. The Bumblebee—so named because of its distinctive yellow and black striped paint job—was a tiny little two-door that barely carried us, let alone enough equipment to stock an undertaking like this.

Between my feet was a small backpack with a change of jeans, some shorts and t-shirts, and three or four changes of socks and underwear. Mick hadn't brought even that much. Both the backseat and trunk were filled with plant starts in little peat pots. They were tall enough to sway back and forth as we drove over increasingly rough roads.

We were jolting along a once-paved back road, listening to Don McLean's *American Pie* album on the 8-track. We chose this tape mostly because it was the only one we had.

"Uh, Mick?"

"Mm-hm."

"You said we were camping up here, right?"

"M-hm."

I glanced into the portable little backseat farm, then back at Mick. "But, we don't have a tent, or food, or… anything, really."

He gave me his trademark Mick smirk, turned the music up louder, and drove into a pothole that reminded me I would need to get my fillings checked as soon as I got home.

Half an hour later, that poor excuse for a road seemed like a dream, as each succeeding turn had brought us onto surfaces that could be called "roads" only by a cock-eyed optimist. Two twin paths marked an avenue for our tires, with long grass growing up between them. Bushes scraped against the doors and windows as we drove.

After another few miles, Mick pulled into an opening between two trees, then drove another hundred feet until we were surround by bushes on three sides. He turned the key, jumped out, and opened the trunk. I pushed the door hard enough against a giant fiddlehead fern to let myself out. "Gotta take a leak?" I asked.

Mick looked surprised. "We're here!"

I looked around. The ruts in the road continued ahead of the Toyota. I had no idea how Mick knew where "here" was.

"C'mon. Grab your shit. We've got a little hike ahead of us."

When I heard Mick say, "a little hike," I envisioned a twenty-mile walk over hill and dale. For once he had been literal and accurate: after a few hundred yards through thick brush, we stepped out into an open meadow. It was mostly flat, with one rising hill in the middle. A large surplus Army tent was pitched to the left of the clearing. What looked like an abandoned shack sat at the edge of the meadow. Green grass and wildflowers covered the ground. Late morning sun shone through the surrounding trees, giving a sun-dappled appearance straight out of a Disney movie. It was the most beautiful place I'd ever seen.

"Is that our tent?"

"Yeah, of course. You didn't think I was going to bring you up here and make you sleep in the dirt, did you?"

"Yeah, maybe."

"I've been coming up here, getting this place ready since spring. Everything's good to go now. We've just got to break ground, get the plants in, then sit around and keep an eye on them while they grow."

I looked around. I couldn't imagine a more remote place. Keep an eye on them against who? How could anyone ever find us and bother our little plants?

"Drop your stuff in the tent, then we can walk out and I'll show you the runway."

I had no idea what the runway was, but I opened the heavy flap and stepped inside. It was warm and smelled like army surplus canvas and unwashed laundry, with a strong chemical finishing bouquet of Cutter's mosquito repellant. Since mosquitoes are the unofficial Alaska state bird, you absolutely, positively, didn't want to leave home without Cutter's. The tent had one cot with a sleeping bag. Next to the cot lay a pile of paperback books and Playboys, and a small bucket filled with cigarette butts and roaches—the discarded joint kind, not the bug kind. On the other side, a rolled sleeping bag sat on a blanket spread on the canvas floor. In one corner sat a disorganized heap of canned food: Dinty Moore Stew, Hormel Chili, and Campbell's soups.

Looks like home. Not bad. I dropped my pack on the empty blanket and went back into the fresh air. Mick was twenty yards away, standing on top of the rise in the middle of the meadow.

"This is gonna be our latrine."

"Why up there?"

"Because there's nothing better than waking up and taking a

shit first thing in the morning, on top of the world."

I had no experience with this idea, but it sounded reasonable.

"C'mon. Grab those stakes and twine, and I'll show you where we're going to work."

A couple of hundred yards north of the camp, we came to a long tree-lined stretch of open grassland. The treetops bent together in the middle to filter the sunshine that fell on the grass. It really did look like a runway.

"Did you build this?"

"God built this. We're just going to borrow it. See how the trees grow? No airplane is going to be able to see what we're doing."

For the first time, it sank in that what we were doing was illegal. I cast a glance over my shoulder, thinking a DEA agent might be waiting for us. "Okay, what do we do?"

"Two inches underneath your tenny runners is good Matanuska Valley soil. We're going to dig and turn the grass and break up the clumps underneath it. Then, we're going to plant our little plants. You won't believe it—they'll grow a couple of inches a day. We'll almost be able to sit here and watch 'em shoot up."

I liked the idea of sitting cross-legged on the ground watching the plants grow. It sounded like contentment. Very Zen. I dropped the cord-wrapped stakes. "What do we need these for?"

Mickey picked up two of them, unraveling the cord. He eyeballed the runway, then pushed one of the stakes into the ground. He walked a straight line and did the same to the other.

"These will measure our beds for us. We're going to be scientific about the way we lay everything out. I know just how much soil each plant needs to grow to maximum size. We'll get started on that tomorrow though. For now, let's go back and dig the latrine."

By the time we got back to camp, I had sweated through my

t-shirt and my throat was burning with thirst. I walked the perimeter of the meadow, looking for a stream to dunk my head in and drink half dry. I found nothing but swaying grass and trees. Mosquitoes were doing the only drinking, having an early Thanksgiving on every inch of my exposed skin. I brought this to Mick's attention, trying not to sound whiny.

Mick stuck his head out of the tent. "Good man. You have identified the one flaw in our little camping Nirvana. There's no fresh water within five miles of here. We've got to pack in everything we drink or use. There's water in a container inside the tent."

Who the hell picks a campsite with no water available? My ever-lovin' brother, that's who. More worried about a great place to grow dope undiscovered than what we're going to drink.

I went inside, found a half-full five-gallon container, and poured some into a dirty plastic cup. It tasted like water with all the life sucked out. It was awful, but I drained it and poured another cup.

"Just remember, we've got to haul back in everything we use. Don't drink too much."

I bit back the reply: *probably not going to be a problem. This isn't exactly an ice-cold Pepsi.*

We exited the tent, grabbed the shovel, and headed to the small rise in the middle of the clearing.

"You want to build, or dig?"

I had no idea what it was we were going to build—I couldn't imagine an outhouse going up here—so I held my hand out for the shovel.

"The hole doesn't have to be too big. Maybe two feet each way. But it's gotta be deep, so we don't fill it up too fast."

Pleasant thought.

I dug. The grass wove itself together into a tight resistance, but as soon as I broke through that, the digging was easy. Mick busied himself chopping down a few saplings at the perimeter of the clearing.

Two exhausting hours later, I was done. When I jumped down in the hole, it came almost up to my armpits. I couldn't imagine that the two of us would poop that much in six weeks. Mick was putting the finishing touches on his creation: a seatless chair, built from saplings and rope. The legs looked too long, but once he pushed them down into the soft soil on either side of the hole, it was just the right height. Mick stood back, admiring his masterpiece. "Whaddya think?"

"I think the first time one of us uses that, we're gonna fall ass first into the hole I just dug."

Mick assumed a look of infinite patience, held up one finger, and retreated to the old shack. A moment later, he reappeared with an old toilet seat. With a little effort, he screwed it where the chair bottom would normally go. "There. A throne fit for a king." Back he went to the old shack, then returned with a lidded bucket. "Lime," he said. "Just sprinkle a little bit each time you use it and you'll never know we've got a shitter right here."

I nodded. I was tired, hungry and worn out. I looked at the sky, which was just as bright as when we had arrived. "What time is it?"

Mick glanced at his watch. "9:30. It gets late fast when it never really gets dark. Come on, let's grab some stew and hit the hay. We've got a busy day tomorrow."

The next few days flew by in a whirl of backbreaking work. We worked at least twelve hours for each of the next few days: turning soil, building beds, and putting the plants in the ground. It was hard, but once my blisters popped and callouses started to form, I loved it. Back home in Mossyrock, life was chaotic. Mom was still a drinking alcoholic, and she and my stepdad fought constantly. Here, in the Matanuska Valley, we saw wildlife every day. No one uttered a cross word, and Mick let me read his

Playboys.

The best thing about the summer was our glorious latrine. Mick had been right. There is nothing better in life than shuffling out of bed, climbing a small hill to sit on a throne made of tree branches, and contemplating the universe and the gorgeousness of your surroundings.

The worst thing was the insect life. I staged an ongoing war with the mosquitoes of the Matanuska Valley. After the first day, when I was essentially one big bite, I religiously applied Cutter's to every inch of exposed skin. That wasn't sufficient, as the little bastards would find a way past the kill zone and work their way inside the band of my jeans or neck of my t-shirt. Eventually, I took to jumping out of my sleeping bag in my underwear and spraying every inch of my body. Twice. Even then, if I missed a spot, they would find it and punish me. One enterprising mosquito managed to crawl inside my sock, all the way to the bottom of my tennis shoe. By the time I noticed, he had feasted on my big toe all day. It was a war I knew I could never win, but I had to fight the best holding action I could.

Once we completed the hard work of breaking ground and planting the seedlings, there wasn't much else for us to do but hang around. Mick wasn't really worried about people stumbling onto our little operation. Natural enemies–rodents, rabbits, or moose–were far greater concerns. Mick thought that if we spent a lot of time around the crop, the animals would be less likely to come around. So far, so good.

At night we sat around a campfire, listening to a battery-operated radio or reading. I remember *Summer Breeze* by Seals and Crofts coming from the tiny speaker while a summer breeze of our own ruffled our hair and cooled us down. For us, it was paradise found.

One night, Mick was tending the campfire while I read one of his Playboys. When I got home, access to a magazine like that would be a long-forgotten dream, so I wanted to absorb as much of it as I could.

"What kind of a car are you going to buy with your share?" he asked.

I contemplated for a moment. "One that runs."

"No, seriously. What kind do you want?"

"Seriously. I just want to not have to ride the bus any more. Anything other than that is a bonus."

"Crazy kids these days," Mick said, shaking his head. As a car nut, he couldn't understand that I just didn't care.

Every three or four days, we would gather up our water containers and make the five-mile drive to the nearest running stream. As soon as the Bumblebee halted, I would jump out, run to the stream and plant my face in it. The stream originated in melting ice and snow; it was shallow, swift, and wonderfully cold. I would drink until my sides ached. I always tried to carry at least a gallon or so of the water the old-fashioned way, inside of me.

After we'd been encamped almost a month, on one of our stream trips, Mick produced a bar of Irish Spring soap and a washcloth. "I don't know what smells worse, the crapper or us, but we're going to do something about our half of the equation."

I gave the stream a doubting look. A foot and a half deep, and freezing cold. What was more, the dirt road ran parallel to the water. We had never seen another vehicle on that road, but it was a road and someone would someday use it. I hung back.

"Don't be a pansy. Come on."

I decided to let Mick show the way. A minute later, Mick was naked and soaping himself up in fast-running water that came just below his knees. I could see goosebumps on his arms, even though it was warm out, and he wasn't dawdling. Stripping down and wading into that water was the second to last thing on earth I wanted to do. Having my brother think I was a pansy was the actual last thing I wanted. I peeled down, piled my clothes, and stepped into the water. It was cold enough to feel like burning. *How the hell did Mick manage to not scream when his toes hit this?*

Like a captured soldier told to march, I took stiff steps until I joined Mick in the middle of the stream. The bastard's malevolent smile told me everything I needed to know. He handed me the slippery bar of Irish Spring and the washcloth; while I did my best to soap up, Mick bent over to rinse by splashing sub-Arctic water on himself.

That was the moment we heard an engine and the sound of tires.

We looked toward the road. There was a Jeep, top down, rolling toward us. Even at a slow pace, it would arrive before we could wade out of the stream and back to our clothes. We both stood there like mannequins, hoping that if we didn't move, whoever was inside the Jeep wouldn't see us.

As it drew closer, we saw two gray-haired ladies inside. They rolled right up in front of us and stopped. The lady in the passenger seat smiled sweetly at us. "Hello, boys. Lovely day for a swim." The Jeep drove away, both its occupants in an uproar of laughter.

Great. No girl has ever seen me naked, but someone my Grandma's age has.

Mick waved at the old ladies, finished rinsing off, and walked back to his clothes. I followed, marveling at his unflappable nature. When we got back to the small piles of clothing, we realized that neither of us had a towel, so we found two big rocks and sat down to drip dry.

A small cloud of mosquitoes formed. *Damn. Washed off 100 layers of Cutter's. Now I've got to start all over again.* Mick pointed to the remnants of a cabin on the other side of the stream. "Do you see where that old shack used to be over there?"

I put my glasses on and squinted. "Yeah."

"That's a bunch of good wood that no one is using."

"I think that depends on your definition of 'good wood,' but okay, yeah."

"I think if we could bring some of that wood back to camp, I could patch that old shack at the campground, and we could stay in there instead of in the tent."

I looked at the stream, which was only a foot deep but about forty feet across, then at the pile of wood. I was never graceful, and I could predict the result of me trying to wade across carrying load after load of lumber. "I'm pretty happy in the tent," I said.

"Listen. I know it will be tough to carry the wood across the stream, so we're not going to do that. Here's what we'll do instead: I'll cross over, pile up the wood we can use, then throw it across to you. Even if it doesn't make it all the way across, you'll just have to wade out and get it. Okay?"

It wasn't okay. I just wanted to fill our water jugs and head back to camp, but in a battle of wills with Mick, I was severely outmanned. Mick got dressed, strung his shoes and socks around his neck, then crossed the stream.

"Oh yeah!" he shouted back at me. "There's a lot of usable wood here. You'll see."

He grabbed a 2 X 4 that was maybe six feet long, walked to the edge of the stream, and threw it. It didn't reach me, but it was close enough that I was able to scramble out without falling and fish it out. I retreated to dry land and tossed it down.

Next was an old piece of plywood, which was much harder for Mick to get a grip on. He did his best to throw it to me, but it caught the wind, kited, and fell to the water closer to Mick than to me. It caught the current just right and disappeared downstream.

"Never mind, there's a lot here. We'll get what we need!"

The third board he threw changed the whole direction of our

summer.

It was another 2 X 4 that looked longer than the first one he'd thrown. He wound up, like a washerwoman emptying a bucket of used water, and let it fly. As the stud fluttered halfway across the stream and fell, Mick screamed and bent double, his hand between his knees. The screaming went on.

"Mick! What happened?" His only answer was a stream of obscenities.

I jumped in the water and ran across the stream, managing not to trip and fall. When I reached the other bank, Mick thrust his right hand at me, gripping it tightly at the wrist with his left. A deep, bloody gash started just beneath his pinky and ran in a jagged line across to his thumb.

I didn't look too closely because I didn't want to see whatever insides the laceration might have laid bare. Instead I looked at the 2 x 4, hung up on some rocks at midstream, and saw a nasty-looking nail sticking out from one end. He had thrown the stud hard enough to rip that wicked-looking piece of rusty metal right through his skin and tissues. We were in the middle of the Matanuska Valley, close to a hundred miles from anywhere, but we needed a doctor.

"Can you drive a stick?" Mick hissed through clenched teeth.

Damn.

The Bumblebee had a manual transmission. Mick's right hand was in no shape to shift gears. I'd had a few lessons in my stepdad's old Courier pickup, so I nodded. Mick was the one bleeding, but I was the one who felt sick.

We picked our way across the running water, found the washcloth we had used, and wrapped it around Mick's hand. I dug around in the back and found an old t-shirt on the floor. I tore strips out of it and did the best I could to bandage his hand, but the blood was already soaking through both layers. We climbed into the Toyota.

I pushed in the clutch, then squinted down at the handle to see if it told me where first gear was.

"I thought you said you could drive a stick?"

"I can. Kind of. Any port in a storm, right?"

"Okay, just give it some gas and start out in second. We're not going to be going fast enough to have to shift out of second until we get back to the highway."

I revved the motor too high, then let the clutch out too slowly. Later than expected, the Bumblebee jerked forward. Somehow the engine didn't die, and we were off like a herd of turtles. It had felt like a long ride on the way out to the campsite, but the ride back was an eternity. Mick dozed off against the passenger side window, and I did my best not to wake him as we herked and jerked down the road.

Anchorage was the closest city, but I had no idea where anything was there, and it was a big city. My stickshift driving was lame enough on back roads and small highways; I didn't want to try real streets with actual traffic. I retraced our path toward Seward without incident or damage, except for potential long-term harm to the clutch, while Mick slept on.

Mick woke up as we came to a stop in front of the apartment. Unless, of course, he had been awake the whole time, but had closed his eyes so he didn't have to watch me drive.

As soon as Joann saw Mick's hand, she hustled him off to the doctor and left me behind at the apartment to wonder how things were back at camp. We had planned to be back in an hour or two. Now we were going to be gone at least overnight. There was nothing electrical to worry about, and we hadn't had a fire going that early in the day, but I still sat and worried about our camp and our little plants.

When Mick and Joann finally got back, his right hand was covered in a bandage so thick it looked like a cast. "Doc says I was lucky. No permanent damage. I'm grounded for a couple of days, then we can go back up."

For two days, I enjoyed the pleasures of mid-1970s civilized living, small-town Alaska style: hot water, television, a basketball court down the street. After a few days, I was antsy to get back to our camp.

The empty water jugs were still in the back, so I filled them up at the apartment and carried them back to the Bumblebee. I stashed a bag of Reese's Cups and Snickers under the seat, hoping they would get me through the last weeks at the campsite, and we took off. Mick drove; neither of us wanted to endure another trip piloted by me. The bandage left the tips of fingers clear enough for him to grasp the Bumblebee's smallish shifter knob.

When we pulled back into our normal parking spot, I felt a grab in the pit of my stomach. "I'll come back and grab the water in a minute," I said. "I want to run ahead and make sure everything's okay with the camp."

I hustled down the small trail between our water source and camp. When I ran into the clearing, the first thing I noticed was how normal everything looked. The throne still ruled its dominion from the hill. The tent was still upright, slowly becoming part of its surroundings. The paperback I had been reading the morning we left to get water—*Ragtime,* by E.L. Doctorow—was still sitting next to the stump I used as a chair.

Worried for nothing.

Mick emerged from the brush, holding his right hand against his chest. He stopped at the edge of the clearing, looked around, and shrugged. "Feel better now? Go get the water, so we can check on the crop."

It took me two trips to carry the water back to camp, but I hurried. I was anxious to see how much the plants had grown in the days we were gone. They had been almost two feet tall when we left, sprouting up like gangly teenagers.

Mick and I walked to the runway. It was a warm July day, and even though the days were getting shorter, we were still getting plenty of sunshine. In July, in the Matanuska Valley, there are only a few hours of night, and they resemble what most of the world describes as dusk.

As we neared the growing beds, Mick said, "Son of a bitch." He didn't say it loudly, but he said it like he meant it.

I squinted at the runway. I could see our growing beds, dark brown against the tan and green of the surrounding grasses.

What I didn't see were the plants.

I broke into a run, but the closer I got, the firmer the truth. The plants were gone.

Mick didn't run. He already knew.

When I got to the first bed, I saw huge cloven hoofprints in the dirt, something like a cow's prints but more than twice the size.

Mick put his left hand on my shoulder and said, "Moose."

I itched to say, "And Squirrel?" in a Boris Badenov accent, but this was not the time, so I stayed quiet.

As we walked the perimeter, it took little forensic effort to piece events together. A moose had wandered into our cannabis buffet. He or she had planted those giant hooves delicately at the edge of each bed and reached a long neck out to pluck and devour each of the plants we had babied along since they were sprouts. The moose had left not a single stem behind.

I looked at Mick, whose eyes were closed. I wondered if he was mentally returning all the things he had planned to buy with his cut of the take. I was doing that with my new car, which had disappeared with a "poof" from my dream.

Mick opened his eyes. First I saw the disappointment in them. Then they cleared. He shrugged and said, "That's that. No time to replant this year. Maybe next year."

Mick got knocked down a lot. Maybe it had made him resilient. I was less so; I stared at the dirt and mourned our plants for a moment. It had been fun planting them, nurturing them. I had never really thought about their end use, nor had I processed the idea of getting paid for the whole project. I had spent a month camping in the Alaska wilderness with my brother. We had sat around a lot of campfires, we smelled terrible, and we had a latrine that offered the best view in the world. It had been a great way to spend the summer.

*****

Back in Seward, I took stock of the situation. Junk food, movies, and comic books had eaten away at my bankroll. I wouldn't even be able to buy my school clothes, let alone dream of getting four-wheeled transportation. Time to adjust.

I called the landlord, my old boss, to see if he had any work. As usual, he had units that needed painting. I spent several of my last days in Alaska that year cooped up in one-bedroom apartments, slapping avocado paint on walls.

I got my final painting payday two days before I was scheduled to fly out of Anchorage. My total bankroll came to $117. With smart shopping, I could afford to get a few pairs of jeans, a couple of new shirts, and some socks and underwear. Thrilling.

That night, as usual, a bunch of people were hanging around Mick's apartment. Mick and Joann were not among them, but that didn't matter. People came and went constantly. I was sitting with three of Mick's crabbing and fishing buddies from the previous season, Jay, Sammy, and Brett. All three were rolling and smoking joints in efficient fashion. By now they all knew I didn't smoke, so no one offered anything to me anymore.

Jay blew a cloud of smoke, then produced a small rubber cup containing dice. "You ever play 4, 5, 6?"

I saw Jay glance over at Sammy. In the corner, two teenage girls sat cross-legged across from each other, knees touching, staring into each other's eyes without saying much. They were only a year or two older than me, but ages ahead in maturity and desirability. I didn't know any of the other people who were in the apartment. "Nope. Don't even know what it is."

"It's a dice game. It's fun. Wanna play?"

"Umm... I guess. Okay."

"Well, you've got to put something into the game to make it fun, but we play for really small stakes. Quarters. Got any quarters?"

I nodded and went up to my room. I closed the door, took out my $117 and change, and laid it on the bed. I put two one-dollar bills and four quarters into my right front pocket. The rest I stuck underneath a book in a nightstand drawer. I was pretty sure I was getting hustled, and I didn't want it to be for very much.

I went back to the living room and laid the dollar bills and quarters on the coffee table.

Jay explained the rules, which were simple. One player served as the banker. He rolled three dice, which resulted in an automatic win, an automatic loss, or a score. If he rolled a score, then the other players also rolled the three dice to try and beat the score. The game is called 4, 5, 6, because that's the best roll you can get. All bets were made before the first roll.

I nodded and put a quarter in front of me. Jay rolled an automatic winner and scooped my quarter over to his bankroll.

I put out another quarter and lost it, too. In just a few shakes of the cup, I was down to my final dollar and congratulating myself for leaving most of my money in the room. "You want me to break that dollar for you, or you want to bet the whole thing?" asked Jay.

I was anxious to let this life lesson play out as quickly as possible, so I said, "I'll play the whole thing."

Jay rolled an automatic loser, and I was halfway back to even. The stakes changed. From then on, we played for folding money.

That automatic loser for Jay was the beginning of the greatest run of luck of my life. 4, 5, 6 is a game of pure luck, not skill, and is simply a matter of how your luck is running. Someone who catches the tailwind of a lot of lucky rolls can go on a streak.

I did.

Within five minutes, I had a nice little stack of singles in front of me. Jay and Sammy seemed to be taking it well. "I knew we shouldn't have started this with you. You're too damn lucky, man."

The girls in the corner continued to sit face to face, oblivious to everything else.

Half an hour later, dollar bets had given way to fives, then tens, and finally twenty dollars per roll. In 1976, twenty bucks was real money, but I was playing with other people's bills. Guys came and went, but I paid no attention. The growing money pile fascinated me. I was also hatching a very real appreciation for the sound those dice made inside that rubber cup. *Roll them bones.*

Soon I had more money than anyone else, and I became the bank. Jay and Sammy busted out, but the dice game took on a life of its own, and I was at the head of it. Players came, dropped a few dollars, and left.

Eventually, I looked up at the clock and saw that it was 4:45 AM. We had been playing nonstop for almost ten hours, and only a few stragglers remained. "I'm sorry, guys," I said. "I'm beat. Anyone else want to be the bank? I'm going to bed."

There were no takers, so I scooped all the money into a pile and carried it to my bedroom. I was too fried to count it, so I smoothed it all into one big pile, folded it over, and stuffed it into my front pants pocket. I fell face first across the bed.

A few hours later, I awoke to Mick pulling on my leg. I felt a pain in my right hip where the bankroll was cutting off the circulation. "Wake up, little brother. I heard you were the big winner last night, so you get to buy all of us breakfast now. How much did you win?"

"No idea." I pulled the money from my pocket and Mick helped me count it.

There was $720 on the bed, plus another $115 in the nightstand drawer. I had never before seen that much money in one place. The day before, I was worried about buying socks and underwear. Now I was once again dreaming of a car.

As custom demanded, I bought breakfast for everyone still in the apartment.

I got on the plane home the next day with an even $800. The flight home felt surreal. I hadn't gotten a good night's sleep since my all-nighter at the dice table, and my head was spinning. As I flew out of Anchorage, I looked down at the snow-capped mountains and smiled inwardly. Throughout the flight, my right hand would drift down to my jeans pocket, verifying that the bankroll was still there.

The first person I saw when I stepped off the plane was Mom. Her hair had been dyed and set at the beauty parlor for her trip to the city.

"Oh, my God, you're still shooting up. You must have grown another two inches while you were gone." She looked appraisingly at my now high-water jeans. "I hope you saved enough money to at least buy yourself some new jeans for school."

"I told you, Mom. I had a job painting apartments." That was true, as far as it went. I pulled out the wad of bills, mostly because I wanted to see her eyes widen.

They did. "Shawn! Did you make all that money just

painting apartments?"
　　I smiled.
　　Some stories are best left untold, at least until a few decades have passed.

Author's Note

Before I get into my thank-yous and acknowledgements, I want to make you an offer. If you'd like to read another book of mine for free, sign up for my New Release Alert List, and I will send you a copy of *Rock 'n Roll Heaven*. I only send an email out when I publish a new book, so you'll only hear from me a few times a year. Of course, I respect your privacy and will never share your email with anyone. If you'd like to sign up for your free copy, you can do that at http://bit.ly/1cU1iS0.

I'd like to thank Doreen Martens for her exemplary work as my editor. She is kind and diplomatic, but most importantly, she catches all my mistakes, both factual and grammatical, and that's no small job. Having her as my editor gives me the confidence to release this book into the wild, knowing it's been well-vetted.

Typically, I only work with one editor per project. However, *My Matanuska Summer* appeared in a previous collection of mine, *Life is Short*. It was edited by J.K. Kelley, who I have worked with on many different projects. As always, he did an outstanding job of making me look good.

In the spring of 2012, I contacted Linda Boulanger and asked her if she would help me design a cover for my very first book. Five years later, and she is still putting up with me and designing beautiful covers. There have been times that we have struggled to find the right cover for a book, but *A Lap Around Alaska* was not one of them. The cover you see here is the first one she showed me. I was only too happy to say "Yes!" Linda also formatted the book, which means she made it look like a book, as opposed to the mess of formatting errors I initially sent her.

I used two proofreaders this time around, because two sets of eyes are always better than mine. I'd like to thank Deb Galvan (who has been proofing for me for what feels like forever) and

Mark Sturgell for catching the remaining slips and goofs that are no doubt placed in the book by gremlins while my back is turned. I appreciate you both making me look much more error-free than I actually am.

I also need to thank my advance readers, who so often give me helpful suggestions and help me form the final book in the earliest stages.

Finally, I'd like to thank you for reading my books and stories. Without you, I'd have no reason to sit down at my keyboard each day.

Shawn Inmon
Seaview, Washington
July 2017

Also by Shawn Inmon

A Lap Around America
Before *A Lap Around Alaska,* there was this book, about a 13,000 mile journey around the back roads of America. Come along with Shawn and Dawn and find America.

Feels Like the First Time
A true love story of loss and redemption, set in the '70s.

Both Sides Now
The flip side of *Feels Like the First Time,* told from Dawn's perspective.

Rock 'n Roll Heaven
Jimmy Velvet dies, but wakes up in the presence of the greatest icons in rock 'n roll history.

Second Chance Love
Steve and Elizabeth were best friends and undeclared lovers, until fate separated them. Twenty years later, they have a second chance, if they are strong enough to take it.

The Unusual Second Life of Thomas Weaver
What if you could do it all again? Thomas Weaver dies, but awakens in his teenage body and bedroom, all memories intact. it.

Life is Short
A collection of 13 short stories that reinforce the idea that life is, indeed, short.

Made in the USA
Middletown, DE
19 April 2022